JANE CUMBERBATCH

sew easy

60 blissfully easy sewing projects for the modern-day homemaker

Special photography by Simon Wheeler
Illustrations by Kate Storer

QUADRILLE

For Alastair, Tom, Georgie and Gracie

Editorial Director Jane O'Shea
Creative Director Helen Lewis
Project Editor Lisa Pendreigh
Pattern Checker Sally Harding
Designer Sue Storey
Illustrator Kate Storer
Production Director Vince Smith
Production Controller Beverley Richardson

First published in 2003 by Quadrille Publishing Ltd, Alhambra House,
27–31 Charing Cross Road, London WC2H 0LS

Cataloguing in Publication Data: a record for this book is available from the
British Library.

ISBN 1 844000 36 2

Printed in China

contents

introduction

Let's get back to basics. As a reaction to the blandness of most mass-manufacture, there's a growing weariness with brand obsession – Nike, Nokia and the latest BMW. Support is increasing for environmentalists and organic protagonists who promote the 'home-made' and 'home-grown' as healthier options for both body and mind, rather than the pre-cooked, shrink-wrapped or ready-made.

There is also gathering momentum against the roller-coaster existence of twenty-first-century life. The idea of embracing home comforts is becoming more appealing. In hip celebrity circles – a good barometer of contemporary trends – it's just as cool to get out the knitting needles and discuss the complexities of purl over plain as it is to rave about your Manolos. It's even okay to admit that you have to dash home early to feed the kids, rather than fib about that 'absolutely vital client meeting'.

E-mail and other technologies that help us to deal with the domestic chores mean that we can pursue our work from home without turning into the kitchen-sink slaves of our mother's generation. Home is an oasis from the big bad world outside, a haven and retreat, and at its most practical a highly efficient workshop, from which is produced food – nothing's more tempting than slabs of home-baked chocolate cake or a garden bursting with lovingly tended vegetables.

My notion is that simple home pleasures are underrated and overlooked in our quick-fix society, in which the media bombards us with the things that we ought to be doing or buying to keep up with the latest trend – an exhausting as well as bank-breaking exercise. Don't get me wrong, I'm the first to drool over a delicious frock from some swanky shop or a gastronomic hit at one of those restaurants where a glass of water costs more than my weekly wine bill, but I'd like to think that it's neither nerdy nor boring to enjoy home sweet home.

This should be heartening for anyone burdened with a large mortgage and demanding children. Which leads me to the observation that making and sewing things has always been an economic move for householders on tight budgets. I learnt all my sewing skills from my mum who grew up with the restrictions of rationing, the 'make-do-and-mend' philosophy imposed by wartime when everything was recycled. She taught my sister and I the basics of stitching and working with paper patterns (the Simplicity range were the best, I remember) from which we constructed rather wobbly edged halter tops, maxi skirts, bellbottom flares and other seventies sartorial necessities.

So this book is all about having a go at being creative and resourceful at home, but without spending an unnecessary fortune or even valuable hours. The satisfaction of having achieved something is another reason why it's fun and stimulating to get out a workbox and sewing machine – far more productive than flopping in front of the widescreen with a take-out pizza.

The ideas in this book are straightforward, stylish and easy. The instructions are simple, too. You don't need a diploma in pattern cutting as with some home-sewing projects. I will show you how easy it is to make simple cushion covers in a gorgeous linen or a filmy curtain with a length of muslin bought cheap in the sales. The budget factor is all important: I use good tough linens and cottons bought as cheaply as I can find them, but if there's some cash left over I will splash out on a gorgeous trimming. (I have a passion for sensual silk and cotton velvet ribbon that can be used to run up a fragrant lavender bag or a simple cushion.)

The key to successful home sewing is not to aim too high or the project will end up as a neglected, half-finished bundle at the back of a cupboard. Think basic – fancy and fiddly pelmets for aspiring interiors are not what this book is about anyway – and remember that the equation is this: simplicity equals style.

Jane Cumberbatch 2003

sew easy essentials

Sew Easy ideas are simple and stylish, and guaranteed to inspire even a beginner sewer. They show you what fun it is run up a cushion or tablecloth in a crisp cotton or to customise a favourite a blanket in need of a revival. *Sew Easy* ideas are the new cool way to prove that originality and stylishness does not have to be purchased from a shop.

Mumsy, earnest, dead boring? No… Pleasure in the simpler things in life can only be a good thing, and with contemporary life under siege from the bland wastefulness of mass manufacture, there is renewed respect for the hand-made and the home-made.

In designing the projects for this book, I have assumed that as a basic sewer you may not be familiar with even the simplest sewing terms and techniques. You're not precluded from using this book if you have no idea how to thread a needle; to make getting started really simple, all of the ideas in this book are based on just a few basic techniques, which are explained on pages 12–15. Much as the most basic home cook can bake a cake or roast a chicken, it is not terribly difficult to master stitching in a straight line using a sewing machine, or if not, be able to hand sew in running stitch.

Sewing, like many skills, is often passed on informally, handed down through generations. Encouraged by the thought of saving himself a fortune, my father taught me to drive when I was 18. Today my 14-year-old son mentors his troglodyte mother at the computer. When you get the sewing bug ask a practically inclined grandma or older sister for help. Haberdashery departments in large stores often have someone to demonstrate how to use a sewing machine and advise on fabrics, or you could enrol on an evening class in basic sewing.

Practice makes perfect. The more you sew the more accomplished you become. If you're a complete beginner, start with something small like the Simple Stitched Table Runner on pages 92–3 before moving on to a larger project.

Shopping for materials aside, most of the ideas in this book can be run up over a weekend. Indeed, some of them, such as the Linen Tea Towel Chair Cover on pages 48–9 or the Appliquéd Daisy Tablecloth on pages 100–101, could be knocked up in a spare hour on a wet Sunday afternoon.

GETTING STARTED

All the pattern pieces in this book are scaled down and are drawn on a grid of squares – each square represents 10cm. The pattern-piece measurements include the seam (and hem) allowances. Most of the patterns have 1cm seam allowances, but hems vary. To make your own paper pattern pieces, draw the shapes on dressmaker's graph paper and cut out. To cut the fabric pieces, pin the paper pieces to the fabric as shown.

Where patterns relate to a specific piece of furniture that you may or may not possess, such as the the Flirty Cotton Chair Cover for the folding cricket chair on pages 42–3 or the Flower Power Chair Cover for the Robin Day chair on pages 46–7 (although both designs are commonplace), use them as a guide to adapting covers for similarly shaped chairs. Another idea is to use an exisiting chair cover and copy it by tracing each pattern piece from the original.

When making up your own pattern, pin newspaper to each section of the chair and draw around the shape to be cut out. Remember to add extra for the seam allowance all the way around each piece.

WORK on a flat surface, such as a large table or floor, ideally with a smooth finish.

PRE-SHRINK your fabric before cutting by washing at the specified temperature.

IRON your fabric before cutting to make cutting easier and more accurate.

LAY OUT all the paper pattern pieces on the fabric following the straight grain, unless they are to be cut on the bias like the Irresistible Silk Nightie on pages 116–17. Pin the pieces in position. If your fabric has a bold print, such as a check or stripe, line up the pieces so patterns will match up.

CUT the fabric carefully around each paper pattern piece.

PIN AND TACK the pieces of fabric together before stitching the seams. Then remove all the pins before sewing.

PRESS all seams flat as you work. If the fabric is delicate, like silk, iron through a clean tea towel. Always iron fabric on the wrong side to avoid shine. Make sure that the setting is correct – high temperatures for linens and cottons, low temperatures for silks and synthetics.

SNIP off all stray thread ends to neaten.

PRESS HEMS on the wrong side of the the item to neaten.

The following basic terms are also useful to know when choosing and using fabric:

SELVEDGE is the woven strip along the two lengthways edges of the fabric.

LENGTHWAYS GRAIN is the fabric warp and runs parallel to the selvedges.

CROSSWAYS GRAIN is the fabric weft and runs perpendicular to the selvedges.

BIAS is the diagonal that intersects the lengthways and crossways grain lines.

GRAINS have different characteristics. The lengthways one has little give, the crossways stretches more, and the bias gives the most.

WORKBOX ESSENTIALS

First, equip yourself a with workbox. I have kept my sewing equipment variously in an old biscuit tin, a drawstring bag run up in some cotton gingham and a wicker basket lined with cotton ticking. Next, invest in a sewing machine – a simple model bought second-hand will suffice for beginners. If you intend to do a lot of sewing, you may want to invest in an overlocker at a later date. Now, you will need to kit out your workbox. Following is a list of equipment you will find useful to have at hand when embarking on a sewing project.

A TAPE MEASURE is essential for sewing purposes, as it can be used for measuring around curves and corners.

DRESSMAKER'S CHALK is for marking fabric – use white for dark fabrics, coloured for patterned fabrics.

PAPER SCISSORS are necessary for cutting paper patterns and templates.

DRESSMAKING SCISSORS have long stainless steel blades and are for cutting out fabric pieces. Keep them sharp.

SEWING SCISSORS are smaller than dressmaking scissors and are useful for trimming seams.

EMBROIDERY SCISSORS with short blades are useful for trimming threads.

DRESSMAKING PINS are rustproof and will not damage fine fabrics.

SHARP NEEDLES are the type you need for general hand-sewing purposes. They come in various sizes. A medium-thickness needle will do for most hand-sewing jobs, but tough fabric like canvas will require a thicker one.

A THIMBLE is a useful tool to protect fingers from needle pricks.

TACKING THREAD is easy to break when unpicking tacking from a piece of stitched sewing. Always use mercerised thread.

SEWING THREAD should always be the same as the fabric – cotton for cotton; polyester for mixed fibres. Use the same colour thread as the fabric. If the fabric is difficult to match, aim for a darker shade.

AN UNPICKER, a little hooked device, is invaluable for undoing stitches and tacking.

A STEAM IRON is a necessity for pressing hems and seams.

AN IRONING BOARD should ideally be a sturdy foldaway shape. Alternatively, lay a thick blanket covered with a sheet on a table for a makeshift ironing board.

A DYE KIT is usually easy to use, but it is essential to read the instructions. I find that machine-washable dyes are best, as you simply put the fabric and dye in a wash cycle, and rinse once afterwards.

TOUCH-AND-CLOSE TAPE is two pieces of fabric – one covered in loops and the other with small hooks – that cling together when pressed. Useful for closing cushions and duvet covers, it is available in different widths and colours and is stitched in place like a ribbon trim.

PRESS-STUD FASTENERS are usually sold with the tool for fixing the studs in place.

BUTTONS are always useful. I have a tin full of assorted buttons, which can also be used to match up with and replace any that fall off. It's also worth looking out for sets of old-fashioned buttons from market stalls.

AN EYELET KIT comes with the appropriate tool to punch a hole and fix the metal eyelets.

FABRIC-COVERED BUTTONS are made with a kit that comes, again, with the necessary tool for fixing.

SAFETY PINS are handy for threading elastic and joining one end to another before stitching or knotting together.

ELASTIC is always useful; I keep a supply of elastic in different widths.

BUYING FABRICS

ASSESS the suitability of your chosen fabric for the project. Is it heavy and opaque enough to cover a thick damask on an old chair? Or is it too fine to suffice as cushion cover and deal with daily wear and tear?

ASK for help. I find that assistants in fabric shops are usually eager to pass on any sewing tips, so make sure you use them.

LOOK at the cut edge of the fabric to see if it frays much. If it does, be prepared to deal with the problem.

WATCH OUT for any flaws. If there are any flaws, you should get extra to make up for the flawed piece. This is particularly important when making large items, when long flawless lengths are required.

CHECK OUT what the fabric is made of, its shrink- and stain-resistant properties and whether it is machine washable or must be dry-cleaned. Buy enough fabric to complete the project. If you go back for more, a new batch will probably not match exactly in colour. For this reason, the amounts specified in *Sew Easy* are generous and will leave a little left over.

my favourite fabrics

My passion for fabrics was planted as a young child. I would trail behind my mum through the local department store, sucking a gobstopper and fingering hand-written swing tickets whilst she investigated the rolls of materials that teetered ceilingwards. I'd earmark cotton with a twee Scottie dog print and persuade mum to run it up into a little skirt on her electric sewing machine. I found the transformation from a limp piece of fabric to wearable item of clothing completely beguiling.

Decades on – as I grapple with making life as simple but as luxurious as possible within limits of budget, time and boisterous children – looking for fabrics is just as thrilling now as it was during those formative suburban shopping expeditions. The most unpromising places can yield star buys: I have leapt on gorgeous blue-and-white checked cottons in modest haberdashery shops; in a pungent Seville side street I discovered fabulous polka-dot fabric, for frilly flamenco dresses, that looks great for retro-style aprons and table linens; and deep inside a dank, chaotic London warehouse a Jewish trader with a heavy Eastern European accent dug out bundles of cheap silks in bright boiled fruit-drop colours.

When buying fabric try not to get carried away. Before parting with any cash there are certain factors worth considering. Is the width of the material compatible with your needs? Is the weight of fabric tough enough for its intended use? Can it be thrown in a washing machine? Will it shrink? Do you mind if the colour fades? If it's a sale length, does it matter if it can't be replaced? I have a store-cupboard of such purchases, that I save up for one-off projects.

CALICO is a plain woven cotton from the eponymous Indian town where it was first manufactured. A wonderful utilitarian fabric with an old-fashioned quality, it comes in

various weights: the thickest makes hardy outdoor awnings and robust chair covers whilst lighter calicos work well as cushion covers and even bedding, in a wide enough width. Be sure to pre-shrink it before use.

CANVAS is a heavy-weight cloth made from from cotton, hemp, flax or jute. It is inexpensive and robust but can be awkward to sew, especially if in large pieces.

COTTON TOWELLING is available in various weights and widths, but you can also simply buy towels to use.

COTTON VELVET comes in wonderful colours such as lime green, shocking pink and purples – more voluptuous and modern than the dingy, mud-coloured velvet drapes that hung in the severe drawing rooms of aged aunts. It's quite expensive but used just for cushions will introduce brilliant shots of colour without breaking the bank.

DENIM COTTON is twilled cotton usually dyed indigo, but there are gorgeous pinks as well. Originally employed as heavy-duty work wear, old Levi Strauss would be tickled to know that denim has endured as a fashion statement. Denim makes good tough chair covers, and is a cool texture for beanbags – the more faded the better.

GINGHAM COTTON is a traditional check that takes its name from ginggang, the Malaysian word for stripe. At home gingham works anywhere, even as just a simple cloth in the most architectural space.

LINEN is spun from flax fibres. With an earthy natural feel, it remains cool on the skin. No wonder colonials wafted through the Empire in the stuff. It comes in various weights and prices, so even the less pecunious can experience its blissful qualities.

MUSLIN is a fine cotton from the East; its name derives from the word 'muslim'. A panel of it fixed to an overlooked window is a more stylish choice than nylon nets. It's a cheap material for floaty curtains, kid's party skirts and jelly bags, which I use when making my yearly batches of quince jelly.

POLYESTER and other synthetics – yes, I know it's very non-PC to use anything other than natural fabrics, but synthetics do have their place in the home, as practical table coverings or outdoor furnishings.

SILK comes thanks to all those worms, who nibble away on mulberry leaves and spin cocoons, which are woven into gorgeous silk finishes. Lightweight habutai silk is perfect for floaty curtains or slinky nightwear. Be careful when stitching it, as it is prone to slipping.

TANA LAWN is a finely woven, smooth cotton. I drool over floral print tana lawns. Tiny bud prints are particularly good for bags, cushion covers and summery halter tops and scarves.

TICKING is a stout twilled cotton closely woven in one-colour stripes on a cream or white background. Traditionally used to cover mattresses, it is easy on the eye. With its simple utilitarian features, it is a favourite of mine for loose covers or cushions.

TRIMMINGS can always be found in my workbox, which contains lengths of cotton broderie anglaise, ribbons, rick-rack and bias bindings in my favourite colours.

WOOL is a natural fibre that breathes, is water resistant and is absorbent inside. Cashmere may be the utlimate, but I prefer the less refined but sensual, comforting qualities of a woolly blanket – the sort we all tucked up in the days before duvets.

tana lawn

gingham cotton

denim cotton

cotton towelling

cotton velvet

silk

tana lawn

tana lawn

polyester

canvas

rick-rack

cotton velvet ribbon

canvas

wool

muslin

calico

ticking

linen

simple sewing techniques

Here are the few basic sewing techniques that you will need to create the *Sew Easy* projects. I have deliberately chosen the simplest sewing methods so that even complete beginners can have a go at making their own groovy creations.

RUNNING STITCH

Secure the thread with a knot or two tiny backstitches. Then make small, evenly spaced stitches along the length of the fabric. Finish with two backstitches to fasten.

TACKING STITCHES

Use long running stitches to hold the fabric in position for final stitching. Start with a knot and leave unfastened at the end. To remove, cut the knot and pull the thread through the fabric from the other end. When tacking delicate fabrics like silk, use a fine thread that won't mark the cloth.

SEAMS

Zigzag stitch along any raw edges to neaten, either before or after joining the seams. Pin and then tack the right sides of the fabrics together. Remove the pins and machine-stitch. Remove the tacking and press the seam open.

HEMS

Turn the hem to the wrong side to the required depth, stitch and press. Alternatively, turn 1cm to the wrong side and press. Then turn the hem over again to the required depth and pin or tack. Stitch close to the first fold. Press.

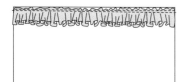

GATHERING

Leaving a long loose thread-end at the beginning, work running stitch along the length of the fabric and secure the end with backstitches. Then slide the fabric along the thread until it is evenly gathered. Secure the loose thread-end by twisting in a figure eight around a pin. Adjust the gathering as required. If attaching a gathered frill, pin or tack the frill to the right side of the fabric and stitch. Topstich along the right side of the fabric, close to the seam, to neaten.

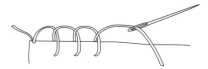

BUTTONHOLES

Mark the position of the buttonhole with dressmaker's chalk. Make the mark a little smaller than the diameter of the button. For machine sewing, work buttonhole stitch along one side following the chalk mark. Then turn to repeat, leaving a small gap as shown. Cut a slit through the gap to make the buttonhole.

BLANKET STITCH

Fasten the thread to the wrong side of the fabric. Insert the needle through the fabric at the desired distance from the edge and bring it up in front of the working thread.

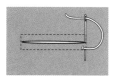

For hand sewing, cut along the length of the chalk mark to open the buttonhole. Then work buttonhole stitch all the way around the opening as shown.

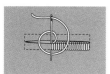

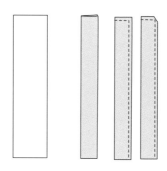

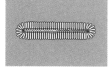

LOOPS AND TIES

Fold the fabric in half lengthways with right sides together and pin or tack. Stitch around two sides leaving one end open. Trim the corner. Turn right side out. Fold inside the raw edges of the open end of ties for neatness before attaching. For pointed ends, stitch and cut at angle as shown.

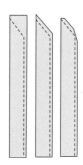

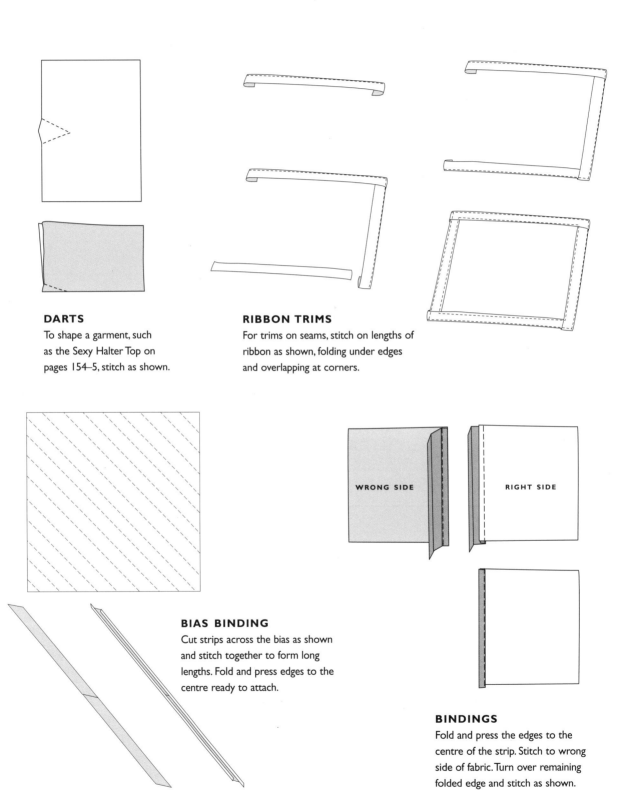

DARTS

To shape a garment, such as the Sexy Halter Top on pages 154–5, stitch as shown.

RIBBON TRIMS

For trims on seams, stitch on lengths of ribbon as shown, folding under edges and overlapping at corners.

BIAS BINDING

Cut strips across the bias as shown and stitch together to form long lengths. Fold and press edges to the centre ready to attach.

WRONG SIDE

RIGHT SIDE

BINDINGS

Fold and press the edges to the centre of the strip. Stitch to wrong side of fabric. Turn over remaining folded edge and stitch as shown.

BINDING A NAPKIN

To make neat corners, stitch on bindings one at a time as shown.

ATTACHING A TRIM

With right sides together, stitch edge of trim to garment. Open out and topstitch along the fabric, close to the seamline.

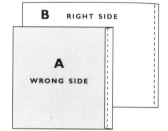

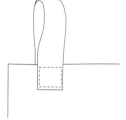

ENVELOPE OPENINGS

Stitch hems on A and B. Overlap B over A and stitch on three sides as shown. Turn right side out.

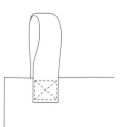

REINFORCED LOOPS AND HANDLES

Attach the loop or handle as shown. Stitch on four sides and then across on both diagonals. Repeat for an extra-secure finish.

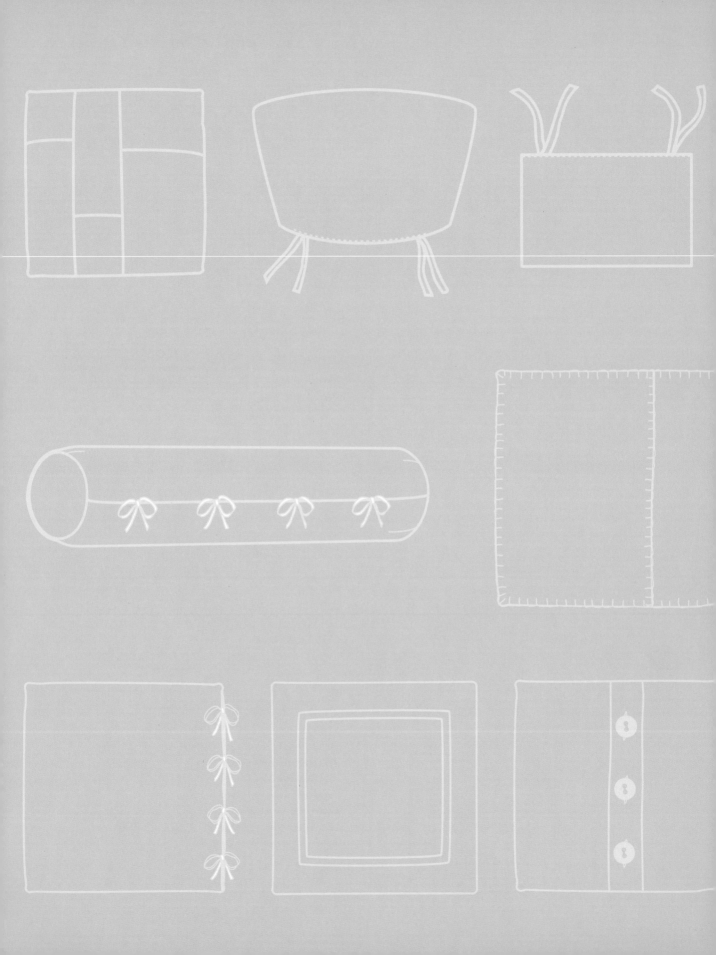

ten essential cushions

CURLING UP IN A CHAIR WITH A PLUMP FEATHER CUSHION IS THE PERFECT WAY TO CHILL OUT.

CUSHIONS, LIKE CLOTHES, SHOULD ADAPT TO DIFFERENT SITUATIONS, EVEN SEASONS. IT ALMOST

GOES WITHOUT SAYING THAT CUSHIONS SHOULD ALWAYS BE MADE WITH GOOD-QUALITY

FILLINGS. TO BE AVOIDED ARE THE UNYIELDING FOAM-ENCASED LUMPS YOU SEE ARRANGED IN

STIFF RANKS IN UPPITY HOTELS.

basic cushion with buttons

Buttoned details are useful fastenings that look neat and crisp – hence city types all buttoned up in their pressed Sea Island cotton shirts and tailored suits. Even though jog tops with zippers are eminently cool, my agnès b cardigans with their school-uniform-like rows of tiny buttons are far more sexy. I wouldn't go so far as to claim the buttoned blue and white checked cushion here is as alluring, but it does have a simple and functional appeal. I recommend that everyone learns to sew on a button at the earliest possible age, if only to avoid detention for sloppy dressing.

MATERIALS

the following makes one cushion cover measuring 53cm by 53cm

70cm medium-weight cotton,
   at least 137cm wide
sewing thread
3 buttons, 3cm in diameter
cushion pad (53cm by 53cm)

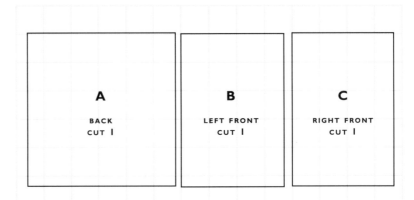

A	B	C
BACK **CUT I**	**LEFT FRONT** **CUT I**	**RIGHT FRONT** **CUT I**

I SQUARE = 10CM

1 Turn and stitch 1cm hem on one long side of B.

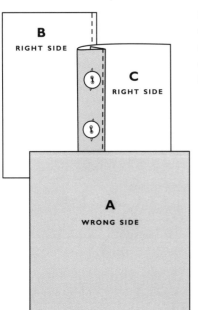

2 To make the buttonhole band on C, turn and press 1cm then 6cm to right side. Pin or tack. Stitch as close to the edge of the band as possible to secure. Stitch and cut 3cm buttonholes as shown (see Simple Sewing Techniques on page 13).

3 With right sides together, layer A, B and C with the hemmed edge of B and the buttonhole band of C overlapping in the centre of A as shown. Pin or tack. Stitch 1cm seam all the way around.

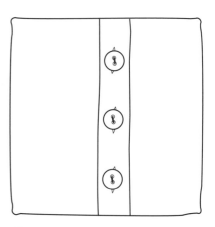

4 Turn cover right side out. Press. Sew buttons to B to align with buttonholes of C. Insert cushion pad.

bolster with side ties

A daybed strewn with classic striped bolsters was the preferred furniture of every typical nineeenth-century heroine. Going for the full period look may be impossible, but if you would like some nice squashy bolster cushions around the place, simply dress them up in any fabric that takes your fancy. A classic striped ticking looks smart because it works well with both plain colours and floral prints. The bolster never goes out of fashion and is one of those useful soft furnishing accessories that looks as good on a sleek modern daybed as it does outside on a plain garden bench.

MATERIALS

the following makes one bolster cover measuring 93cm long and 25cm in diameter

120cm medium-weight cotton
   ticking, at least 137cm wide
sewing thread
2m grosgrain ribbon, 17mm wide
cushion pad (93cm by 25cm diameter)

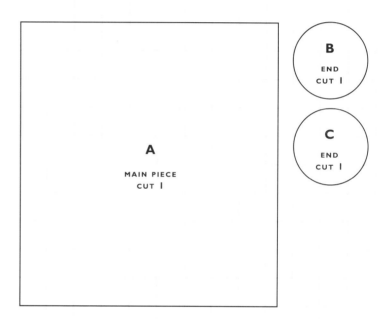

A
MAIN PIECE
CUT 1

B
END
CUT 1

C
END
CUT 1

1 SQUARE = 10CM

1 Turn and press 1cm then 2cm to wrong side on both short sides of A for hems. Stitch in place.

2 With right sides together and hemmed edges if A overlapping, pin or tack one long side of A to the circumference of B. Stitch 1cm seam. Repeat on other side with C.

3 Turn cover right side out. Press. Cut eight 25cm lengths of ribbon and stitch in pairs on both sides of cover opening.

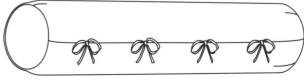

4 Insert cushion pad. Tie ribbons in bows to secure.

blanket-stitched cushion

Here I am in recycle mode again and extolling the virtues of second-hand shops and sales, where you are much more likely to come across interesting retro sixties prints, fabulous old linens, pretty quilts and faded blankets. Even moth-eaten and worn items are worth buying as you can chop out and use the best bits. This woolly cushion made from a recycled blanket decorated with traditional blanket stitch in a bright pink wool looks good in any interior and is the perfect partner for a post-lunch snooze.

A
FRONT
CUT 1

B
BACK
CUT 1

C
BACK
CUT 1

1 SQUARE = 10CM

1 Using a length of wool yarn, work blanket stitch along stitch one long side of B.

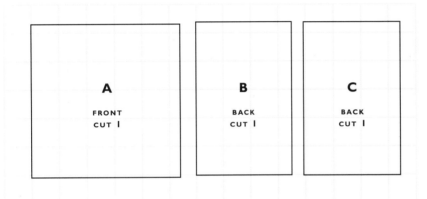

 MATERIALS
the following makes one cushion cover measuring 53cm by 53cm

70cm by 150cm piece cut from an
    old blanket
sewing thread
wool yarn for blanket stitch
darning needle
cushion pad (50cm by 50cm)

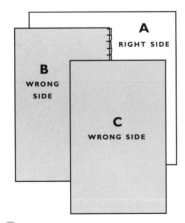

2 With right sides together, layer A, B and C with the blanket-stitched edge of B overlapping C in the centre of A as shown. Pin or tack. Stitch 1cm seam all the way around.

3 Turn cover right side out. Press. Work blanket stitch around all edges. Insert cushion pad.

velvet-trimmed cushion

I once spent hours grappling with mitred corners after thinking it would be a good idea to sew some Oxford pillowcase-style cushions for my sofa. Never again. So I am pleased to say that I have discovered the cheat's way to make this floppy edged cushion cover trimmed with delicious powder blue velvet ribbon. There's no need to go to all the fuss and bother of measuring angles as all that's needed is a quick circuit of machine stitching around the cushion cover to produce the required effect.

MATERIALS
the following makes one cushion cover measuring 70cm by 70cm, including border

180cm linen, 90cm wide
2.3m cotton velvet ribbon, 2.5cm wide
sewing thread
cushion pad (52cm by 52cm)

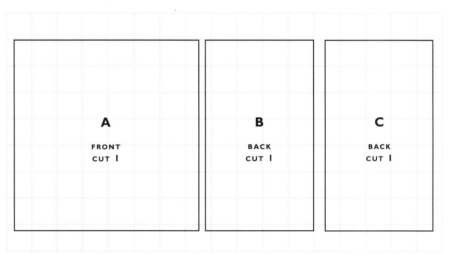

A

FRONT
CUT 1

B

BACK
CUT 1

C

BACK
CUT 1

I SQUARE = 10CM

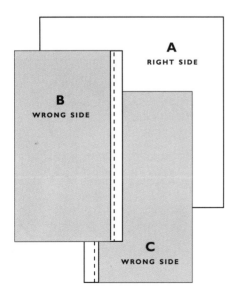

A

RIGHT SIDE

B

WRONG SIDE

C

WRONG SIDE

1 Turn and stitch 1cm hem on one long side of both B and C. Press.

2 With right sides together, layer A, B and C with the hemmed edges of B and C overlapping in the centre of A as shown. Pin or tack. Stitch 1cm seam all the way around.

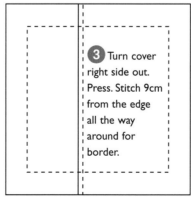

3 Turn cover right side out. Press. Stitch 9cm from the edge all the way around for border.

4 Cut four 56cm lengths of ribbon and stitch to the front as explained on page 14, just outside the stitched border. Press. Insert cushion pad.

patchwork cushion

It doesn't matter how many different patterns you use when putting together patchwork as long as you settle on a colour theme. However, it is helpful if you have an even balance of plains with large and small patterns to help the visual diversity of the patchwork surface. As a 10 year old I sweated over a patchwork pillowcase in fiddly hexagonal shapes, that was destined never to be finished. I learnt that simpler tricks such as making patchworks with rectangles and squares sewn together in strips is far more productive.

✳ As this is a patchwork, remember all C pieces will be cut from varying fabrics

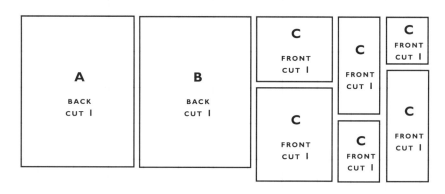

I SQUARE = 10CM

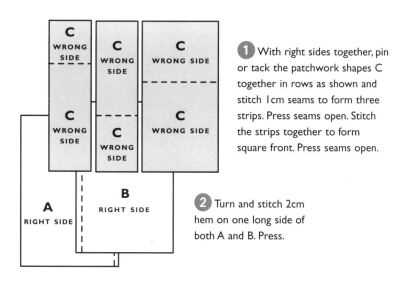

1 With right sides together, pin or tack the patchwork shapes C together in rows as shown and stitch 1cm seams to form three strips. Press seams open. Stitch the strips together to form square front. Press seams open.

2 Turn and stitch 2cm hem on one long side of both A and B. Press.

3 With right sides together, layer A, B and C with the hemmed edges of B and C overlapping in the centre of A as shown. Pin or tack. Stitch 1cm seam all the way around.

 MATERIALS
the following makes one cushion cover measuring 41cm by 41cm

remnants from your workbag sewing thread

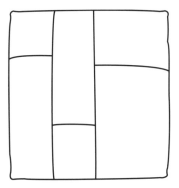

4 Turn cover right side out. Press. Insert cushion pad measuring 41cm by 41cm.

roll-up beach mattress

Any beach babe or boy knows that a certain amount of kit is needed for a day soaking up the rays or riding the surf: protective umbrella, coolbox, gripping novel and money for ice-creams, plus something appealing to lie on. In my youth we dragged plastic lilos down to the sands for a bit of comfort, but it was hard work blowing them up and they had an irritating tendency to puncture easily. Inspired by the Japanese futon, this lightweight roll-up mattress is ideal for beach use or for lounging on at the local outdoor pool. It can, of course, be thrown in the washing machine.

MATERIALS

the following makes a mattress measuring 66cm by 166cm

190cm heavy-weight cotton, at least 140cm wide
two pieces cotton wadding, 62cm by 162cm, 2.5cm thick
sewing thread and cotton yarn, for knotting
3.2m linen tape, 2.5cm wide, for ties

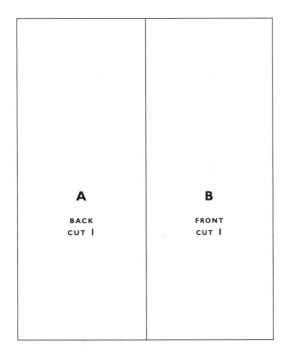

I SQUARE = 10CM

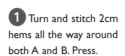

1 Turn and stitch 2cm hems all the way around both A and B. Press.

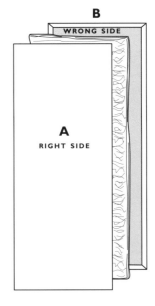

2 Cut 2 layers of wadding, each 2cm less all the way around than the hemmed pieces A and B. Sandwich the wadding between the wrong sides of A and B. Pin or tack.

3 Stitch 1cm from edge all the way around A and B to enclose the wadding.

4 Using a darning needle, sew 15cm doubled lengths of cotton yarn through the layers of the mattress. Knot and cut to desired length.

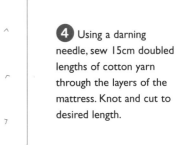

5 To make the ties, cut two 160cm lengths of linen tape and sew to one end of the mattress. Make one side of the length longer than the other (120cm and 40cm).

tie-on chair cushions

Tie-on flat cushions filled with wadding, or squabs as they are also known, will give extra support and comfort to chairs if they are used for eating and therefore require the sitter to be in one position for long periods. They are also a good excuse to play around with fabrics in great colours or patterns such as this sixties-inspired spot print, which goes perfectly with the geometric wire structure of a market-find Bertoia chair.

MATERIALS

the following makes a chair-back cushion 28cm by 42cm and a seat cushion 55cm wide at front and 42cm wide at back and 35cm deep

110cm medium-weight cotton, at least 137cm wide
cotton wadding, 100cm by 70cm and 1cm thick
sewing thread

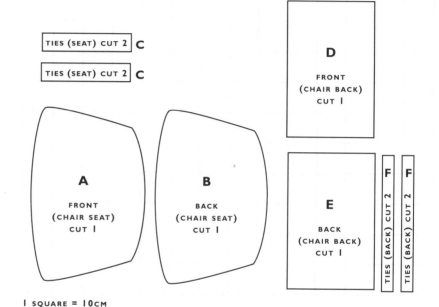

I SQUARE = 10CM

1 With right sides together, pin or tack A to B. Stitch 1cm seam around three sides as shown. Repeat with D and E.

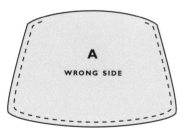

2 Turn covers right side out. Press. Cut two pieces of wadding for each cushion, each 2cm less all the way around than A/B and D/E. Insert wadding. Fold 1cm to the inside around the opening of both covers and pin.

3 Make two sets of ties for both seat and back cushions (see Simple Sewing Techniques on page 13). Insert appropriate ties into seat and back covers where shown and pin or tack. Stitch opening close to the edge to secure.

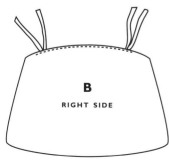

denim cotton pouffe

Found in posh houses and suburban semis alike, the pouffe is a familiar object across the entire social spectrum. It has a multitude of uses such as perching on in front of the TV or putting up one's feet. Seen here is a modern take on this useful little accessory in a bright pink denim. If making several, go to a wholesaler to buy the fabric and polystyrene stuffing so this becomes a cheap solution for low, informal seating.

MATERIALS
the following makes one pouffe 41cm in diameter and 36cm high

100cm cotton denim, at least 137cm wide, for the outer cover
100cm calico, at least 137cm wide, for the inner bag
sewing thread
foam, feathers or polystyrene balls, for stuffing

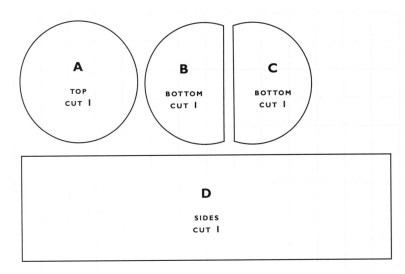

A
TOP
CUT 1

B
BOTTOM
CUT 1

C
BOTTOM
CUT 1

D
SIDES
CUT 1

1 SQUARE = 10CM

1 Turn and stitch 1cm hem on straight edges of B and C. Press.

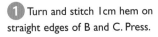

2 Overlap hemmed edges of B and C to form a circle the same size as top A. Pin or tack top and bottom edges to secure.

3 With right sides together, stitch short ends of D together with 1cm seam. Press seam open.

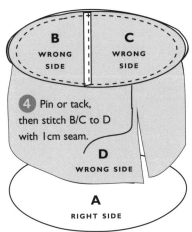

B
WRONG SIDE

C
WRONG SIDE

4 Pin or tack, then stitch B/C to D with 1cm seam.

D
WRONG SIDE

A
RIGHT SIDE

5 Stitch D to top A in the same way.

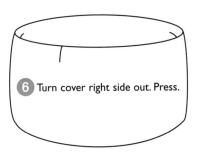

6 Turn cover right side out. Press.

7 Using the calico, make the inner bag in the same way, but replace pieces B/C with another full circle as A. Leave a small opening to stuff the inner bag with the filling. Once stuffed, stitch gap to close and insert in cover.

frilly edged cushion

A frilly cushion can either look naff, as in bed-and-breakfasts where nylon sheets and cushions crackle with static, or it can look sweet and rather stylish. The key, of course, is in choosing the correct balance of fabric, texture, colour and pattern. Lightweight tana lawn cotton with a small floral print for the frill and a larger one for the main cushion – such as the Liberty print here – work well. Alternatively, try the same idea using ginghams or spots with florals. Soften the sugary look by using frilled details against starker elements such as plain white covers and modern metal chairs.

MATERIALS

the following makes one cushion cover measuring 40cm by 40cm

60cm tana lawn cotton, at least 137cm wide
60cm tana lawn cotton, at least 137cm wide, in a contrasting print for frill
sewing thread
cushion pad (40cm by 40cm)

A	B	C
FRONT CUT 1	BACK CUT 1	BACK CUT 1

D FRILL CUT 1

D FRILL CUT 1

D FRILL CUT 1

D FRILL CUT 1

1 SQUARE = 10CM

1 Turn and press 1cm then 3cm to the wrong side on one long side of both B and C for hems. Pin or tack. Stitch in place.

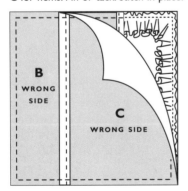

B WRONG SIDE

C WRONG SIDE

2 With right sides together, stitch narrow ends of D together with 1cm seams to make one continuous band. Press seams open. Fold D in half lengthways with wrong sides together. Press. Gather frill D to fit all the way around A (see Simple Sewing Techniques on page 13). Pin or tack frill D around the edges of A with right sides together.

3 With right sides together, layer A, B and C with the hemmed edges of B and C overlapping in the centre of A as shown. Pin or tack. Stitch 1cm seam all the way around.

4 Turn cover right side out. Press. Insert cushion pad.

cushion with side ties

You can't go wrong with creamy coloured heavyweight cotton to make up robust cushion covers that can be washed and washed again. The simple tie detailing of cut lengths of linen tape (available from dressmaking shops and haberdashers) could be varied with bright coloured ribbons or ties.

MATERIALS

the following makes one cushion cover measuring 52cm by 56cm

70cm cotton drill, at least 137cm wide
sewing thread
2.4m linen tape, 1cm wide, for ties
cushion pad (52cm by 56cm)

A
FRONT
CUT 1

B
BACK
CUT 1

1 SQUARE = 10CM

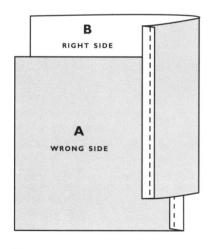

B
RIGHT SIDE

A
WRONG SIDE

1 Turn and stitch 3cm hem on one short side of both A and B.

3 Turn cover right side out. Press. Cut eight 30cm lengths of linen tape for bows and stitch to both sides of opening at equal intervals as shown. Insert cushion pad.

2 With right sides together and B folded around A, pin or tack in place. Stitch 1cm seam around three unhemmed sides (see Simple Sewing Techniques on page 15).

smart ideas for cushions

ten tips for chilling out

❶ Take the phone off the hook and then put your feet up with a glass of ice-cold bubbly that you cleverly put in the freezer one hour earlier.

❷ When my mind is racing and intense novels are too much to concentrate on, I turn to my crime pile. Mankell, the Swedish crime author who was brought to my attention by a publisher friend, has a gripping list of psychological thrillers, and nothing beats Agatha Christie for some good old-fashioned plots and murders.

❸ Eat some chocolate. According to experts, it apparently raises serotonin levels and improves your mood. I'll buy that.

❹ Bring out the artist in you. Buy a tin of really good colouring pencils and a pad and have a go at sketching or colouring your designs.

❺ Make a list of things that need doing. Even if life is chaotic crossing off one task a day will make you feel more in control.

❻ If you're lucky enough, light a fire and tuck up with a woolly blanket. Warmth and blazing flames have a wonderfully calming effect on the soul.

❼ Listen to a play on the radio or a book on tape, it's so much soothing than chasing your eyes across a screen.

❽ Phone your best friend for a gossip. It's better than any therapist for getting things off your chest and realising that you're not the only one feeling useless.

❾ Paint your toenails with something pink and flamboyant.

❿ Plan your next birthday party.

ARE YOU SITTING COMFORTABLY?

Cushions are tremendously adaptable, and making them is one of the cheapest ways to add colour and texture to rooms, even if you are on a tiny budget. At one end of the scale, with payment for a job safely in the bank you might be considering a new look for a sofa with a new loose cover in a gorgeous cream linen and piles of squashy cushions in your favourite vintage fabrics. If funds are continually stretched, it's worth building up a bag of remnants – a pair of velvet curtains or an old cotton tablecloth in country checks could be cut up and re-used. In fact, any fabric item in colours and textures that you like can be saved to run up some new cushion covers when needed. For examples of stylish recycling, see the Blanket-stitched Cushion on pages 22–3 and the pretty Patchwork Cushion on pages 26–7.

HANDY HINTS FOR CUSHION STUFFINGS

Interior decorators of the old school have very particular ways of doing things. I once knew a white-haired tartar who would send her minions scurrying with her plummy authoritative tones and boss her clients into metres of flowery chintz for elaborate swagged and draped hangings. So finely honed was her commercial nose that all the furniture in her house had price tags on it. 'Cushions,' she would bark, 'should be properly stuffed with feathers.' The mere mention of foam chips would send her into apoplexy. I have to say that I absolutely agree with her, having lived in enough cheap rented flats with hideously uncomfortable, tea-stained, foam-encased upholstery – we would have burnt to crisp if there had ever been a fire. There are, however, occasions when synthetics can be used to good effect and many are now fire-proofed.

POLYSTYRENE BEADS for stuffing bean bags can be bought in big bags from fabric wholesalers, but should be poured into an inner lining before stuffing a bean bag floor cushion.

FOAM RUBBER can be bought in different thicknesses and cut to size. It is resilient and useful for stuffing outdoor mattresses for the beach and the poolside.

WADDING in a light weight is a good idea for stuffing seat pads and for portable beach rolls – see the Roll-up Beach Mattress on pages 28–9. It can be used in layers if a greater thickness/weight is required.

FASTENINGS good for cushions are zippers or buttons, but for less sewing and fuss, consider simple envelope openings and ties.

CLEANING YOUR CUSHIONS

Ideally, cushion covers covering a feather cushion pad should be removeable and washable. For accidents and emergencies, see the guide to removing spots and stains from fabrics on pages 86–7. And don't fret, daily plumping of cushions isn't a sign that you've got an obsessive problem. It's just a practical means of keep the feathers distributed evenly and keeping your cushions in good shape.

ENJOYING YOUR CUSHIONS

Don't get me wrong. I'm not advocating a couch-potato diet of TV soaps, velour tracksuits and pizza slices. As the media has splurged with heaven knows how many health gurus and lifestyle advisors, there's no excuse for this type of flabby existence. Similarly, it's just as toxic at the other end of the scale, when straining to be a domestic goddess is more like being a rollerskater on speed with barely a moment to breathe let alone snatch some me-time (nigh on impossible for anyone with a brood of children and a job).

CHILL OUT WITH A CHOCOLATE, CHESTNUT AND ORANGE SLAB

Here's the recipe for my favourite chocolate, chestnut and orange slab – a flavour and texture combination where the ingredients are made for each other. This recipe, I assure you, will have everyone drooling and asking for more.

FOR THE CAKE	FOR THE ICING
400g peeled chestnuts	125g chocolate
125g caster sugar	(minimum 70% cocoa solids)
125g chocolate	15g butter
(minimum 70% cocoa solids)	15ml fresh orange juice
100g butter	15ml grated orange rind

Place the peeled chestnuts and sugar in a food processor and whizz until smooth. Cut the chocolate and butter into small pieces and melt in a large saucepan. Add the chestnut and sugar paste to the chocolate and mix until smooth. Turn into a greased cake tin and chill in the fridge overnight.

To make the icing, melt the chocolate with the butter, orange juice and rind and stir until smooth. Spread over the slab and leave to set in the fridge. Cut into slices before serving.

ten tips for going green

❶ Preserve the earth's water supplies by taking a shower rather than a bath. As well as leaving you feeling refreshed, a shower uses three times less water.

❷ Fit energy-efficient light bulbs in your home. They last eight times as long and use one-fifth of the energy of standard ones.

❸ Insulate your loft at home and you could save a substantial amount each year on your heating bills.

❹ When you finish off a shop-bought preserve, keep all the glass jars for your annual batch of home-made marmalade. For every tonne of glass recycled a tonne of raw material is saved.

❺ Send your tin cans to be recycled. Cans made from recycled aluminium use 95 per cent less energy than those made from scratch.

❻ Resist fuel-wasting exotic fruits and vegetables flown in from distant parts and stick to fresh seasonal local produce.

❼ Re-use envelopes. When this isn't possible, always look for paper products made from sustainable sources.

❽ Walk. Don't take the car. It's much healthier for you and the environment.

❾ Send any unwanted gifts and old clothes to charity shops.

❿ Visit the same charity shops to pick up a bargain.

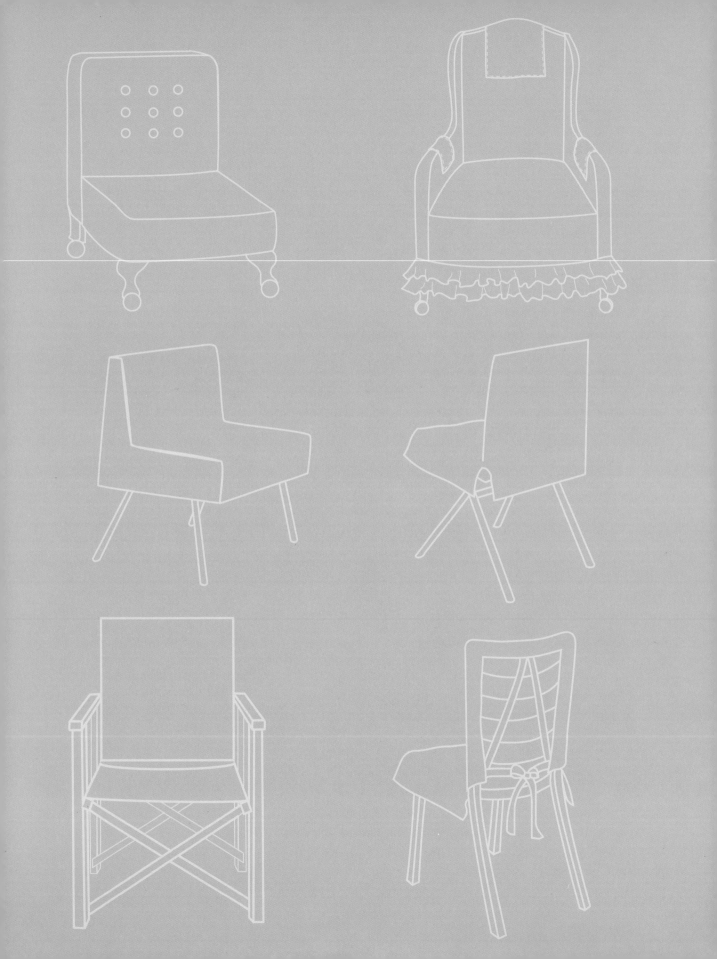

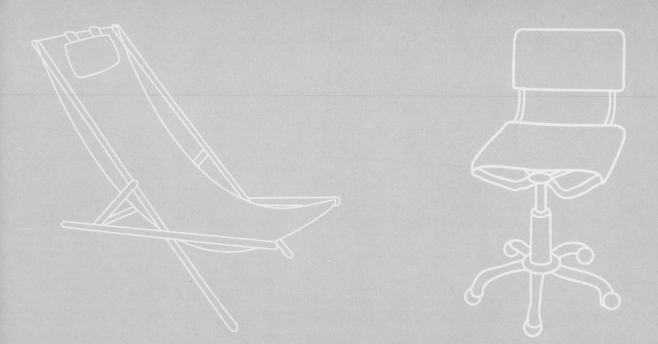

ten essential chair covers

TEN SIMPLE IDEAS TO UPDATE BASIC CHAIRS — FROM A CRISP BLUE AND WHITE LINEN TEA TOWEL CLEVERLY USED TO CREATE A NEAT APRON-STYLE COVER TO LIME GREEN COTTON RUN UP TO MAKE A FRILLY PULL-ON SHAPE FOR A BASIC FOLDING CHAIR. ALL ARE EASY TO ADAPT FOR YOUR OWN CHAIR WITH THE MINIMUM OF ANGST REQUIRED ON THE PART OF THE SEWER.

flirty cotton chair cover

Dress up a garden chair, or any other junk chair that needs a little help, with a simple flirty cotton chair cover secured with bows tied at the sides. The shorter and more gathered the frill, the perkier it looks. It's best to use a lightweight cotton, as a heavy canvas or velvet, for example, will not give the same light and flounced effect.

MATERIALS

the following makes a cover for a garden chair

170cm lightweight cotton, at least 90cm wide
sewing thread

1 SQUARE = 10CM

1. Turn and stitch 1cm hems on both short sides and one long side of C (if the long side has a selvedge, you can omit the hem). Press. Gather the unhemmed side of C to fit along the top of A as shown (see Simple Sewing Techniques on page 13).

2. With right sides together, pin or tack the gathered side of C to the top of A. Stitch 1cm seam.

3. Fold A where shown to fit over back of chair, placing right sides together. Stitch 1cm seams along sides of A. Turn cover right side out. Press.

4. Make ties D (see Simple Sewing Techniques on page 13) or use two lengths of ribbon. Attach to A as shown.

5. Hem and gather B as for C, but to fit around the three sides of A as shown.

6. With right sides together, pin or tack the gathered side of B around the three sides of A. Stitch 1cm seam. Press.

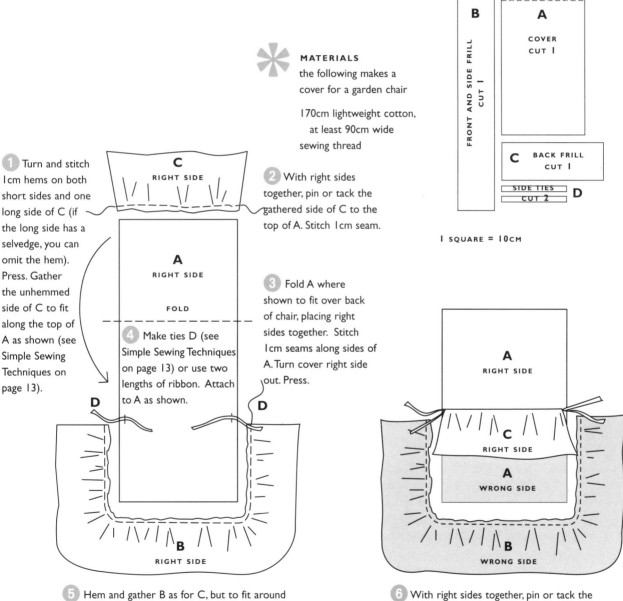

deckchair pillow

Nothing beats a traditional deckchair covered in a bold striped canvas for summer lounging by the sea or in the back garden. Add to the comfort factor with a detachable soft towelling pillow on which to rest your sleepy head. When fixing canvas to a deckchair, you can either stitch it in place around the frame (in which case, remove the sewing machine's needle beforehand in order to position the frame and fabric) or you can wrap the top and bottom of the canvas around the frame and secure it with a row of tacks, using a hammer to bang them in place.

MATERIALS

the following makes one pillow measuring 21cm by 29cm

60cm cotton towelling, at least 70cm wide
wadding, 25cm by 60cm wide and 2.5cm
   thick
sewing thread
press-stud kit (available from hardware
   shops or department stores)

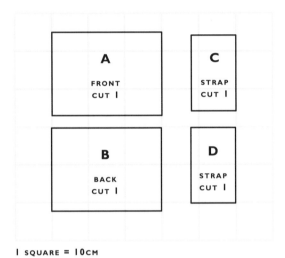

I SQUARE = 10CM

1 With right sides together, pin or tack A to B. Stitch 1cm seam around three sides as shown. Turn cover right side out. Cut two pieces of wadding each 1cm less all the way around than A/B. Insert wadding.

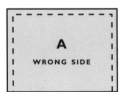

2 Fold strap C in half lengthways with right sides together and pin or tack. Stitch 1cm seam along long side and one short side.

3 Turn C right side out. Attach two press studs to sewn ends of strap. Repeat steps 2 and 3 with D.

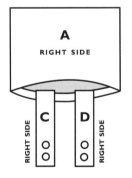

4 Fold 1cm to the inside around the opening of A/B and pin. Pin or tack unsewn ends of C and D between A/B where shown. Stitch the opening as close to the edge as possible.

5 Attach press studs to back of deckchair to correspond to those on straps.

flower power chair cover

Running up a simple cover in floral print cotton is a very good way of making a beaten-up chair rescued from the dump look a million dollars. But then this little chair is not without its own design pedigree being one of the many thousands that were produced during the sixties to a design by Robin Day. Once standard issue in offices and schools throughout the country, they can now be picked up quite cheaply in secondhand office furniture shops. Keep the hemline high to make the most of the chair's good-looking legs.

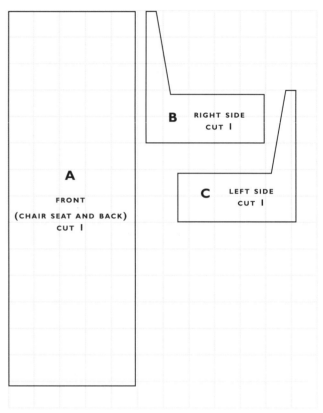

I SQUARE = 10CM

1 With right sides together, pin or tack A to B and C as shown. Stitch 1cm seams.

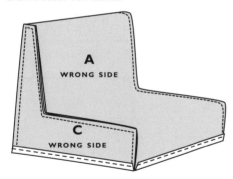

2 Turn and stitch 1cm hem all the way around bottom edge, undoing the hem seams at the corners if necessary. Turn cover right side out. Press.

MATERIALS
the following makes a cover for an average-size chair

160cm floral print cotton, at least 112cm wide
sewing thread

linen tea towel chair cover

Although the linen tea towel — or glass cloth as it is known in more traditional circles — is usually employed to buff glasses to a sparkling sheen, it is also a very versatile kitchen accessory. Inspired by restaurant staff who tuck tea towels into their waistbands as makeshift aprons, I came up with this very simple idea using a linen tea towel and white cotton tape to make an apron for a chair. Dress up all your mis-matching kitchen chairs to turn your surroundings into something altogether more stylish. When the covers need a wash, just chuck them in the washing machine.

MATERIALS

the following makes a cover for an average-size kitchen chair

linen tea towel, measuring
    85cm by 60cm
2m cotton tape, 2.5cm wide
sewing thread

1 Cut two 10cm slits into the tea towel where cover will bend up from seat to chair back. Turn and stitch narrow hems on raw edges of slits as shown below left.

2 Press 5cm to wrong side on both sides of tea towel abovehemmed slits. Stitch across this turnback 5cm from top as shown.

3 Fold the cotton tape in half and attach to the top of the tea towel in the centre as shown.

4 Press 5cm to wrong side at top of tea towel. Stitch this turnback to the first turnback at corners, but do not stitch through the front.

5 Attach the cotton tape to the sides of the tea towel just above the hemmed slits as shown.

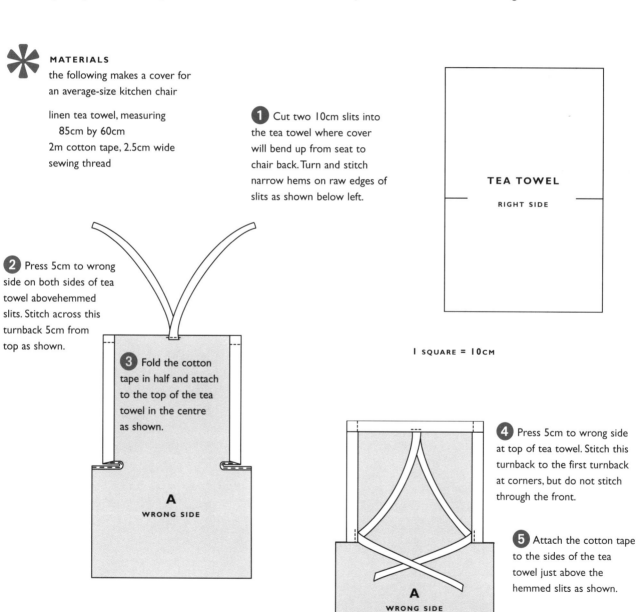

TEA TOWEL

RIGHT SIDE

1 SQUARE = 10CM

A
WRONG SIDE

A
WRONG SIDE

canvas director's chair cover

In outdoor furniture catalogues, the classic folding director's chair is frequently marketed as if it had just left the set of Out of Africa, with neutral-coloured covers with names like 'Savannah' or 'Bush'. To make this very adaptable, timeless chair a far more exciting animal, I have taken off the old covers and replaced them with turquoise-green canvas edged with a smart blue ribbon trim.

MATERIALS

the following makes a back and seat for a small director's chair

60cm canvas, at least 137cm wide
2.4m grosgrain ribbon, 5cm wide
sewing thread

1 Bind both long edges of A and B with grosgrain ribbon (see Simple Sewing Techniques on page 14).

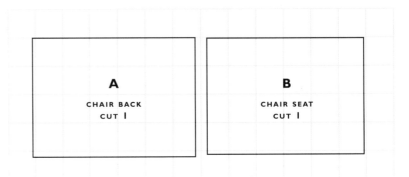

A
CHAIR BACK
CUT 1

B
CHAIR SEAT
CUT 1

1 SQUARE = 10CM

A
RIGHT SIDE

B
RIGHT SIDE

2 On both unbound sides of A and B, turn 1cm to wrong side and pin or tack into place.

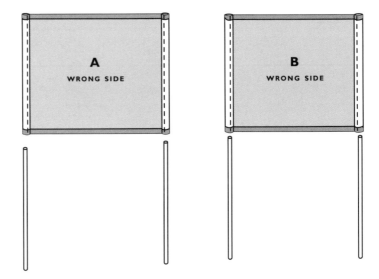

A
WRONG SIDE

B
WRONG SIDE

3 Turn hem under again to form a channel large enough to accommodate the chair rods. Stitch in place. Insert the rods of the chair as shown. Slide covers into position on the chair.

groovy office chair cover

Even if your salary isn't megabucks and your eyes are swimming from staring at a computer screen, improve your well-being at work by dressing up a standard-issue office chair with this luxurious hot pink cotton velvet chair cover. The fabric isn't cheap, but under a metre is enough. A word of warning: mouse pinks and drab greys definitely lean towards bank-manager style and so should be avoided. (No offence to any groovy bank managers out there.) Stick to colours that sing, like lime green or sky blue.

MATERIALS
the following makes a cover for
a small office chair

70cm cotton velvet, at least
 112cm wide
2.4m ribbon, 1cm wide, for ties
sewing thread

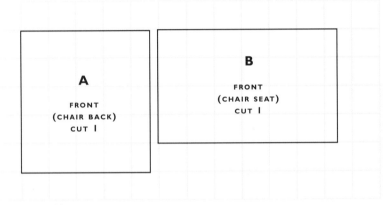

A
FRONT
(CHAIR BACK)
CUT 1

B
FRONT
(CHAIR SEAT)
CUT 1

1 SQUARE = 10CM

1 Fold A in half widthways with right sides together and pin or tack. Stitch 1cm seam along both short sides of A.

A
WRONG SIDE

2 Turn and stitch 1cm hem all the way around opening on A. Turn cover right side out. Press.

3 Turn and stitch 1cm hems on all sides of B, taking care when overlapping the hems at each corner.

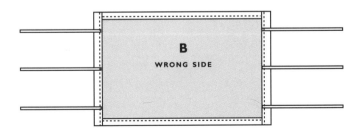

B
WRONG SIDE

4 To make ties, cut six 40cm lengths of ribbon and stitch to wrong side of B at regular intervals as shown.

fluffy towelling chair cover

It's quite amazing what you can do with just one bath towel, as I discovered when covering a little folding cricket chair for the bathroom – of course, this idea will work anywhere in the house. How about a set of dining chairs in natty blue and white stripes for outdoor summer parties. You could run up a set of these covers in no time at all, as there's barely any sewing to be done because the towel is already finished on all sides.

MATERIALS
the following makes a cover for a small, thin-backed chair

1 bath towel, measuring 140cm by 70cm
sewing thread

1 Trim the sides of the towel to size, as shown. Cut two slits into the towel where indicated. Overlock or zigzag stitch all raw edges including the slits.

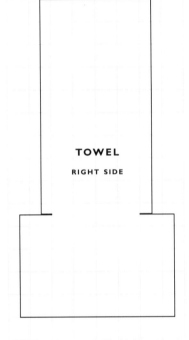

TOWEL

RIGHT SIDE

1 SQUARE = 10CM

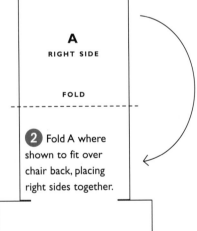

A

RIGHT SIDE

FOLD

2 Fold A where shown to fit over chair back, placing right sides together.

3 Pin or tack along sides of A from fold to the slits. Stitch 1cm seams. Turn cover right side out.

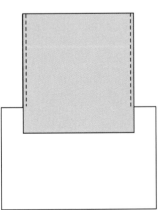

pull-on chair cover with buttons

This loose cover in calico is designed for a chair without arms, which leads me to confess that I decided to omit a pattern for a traditional loose armchair cover as, for many beginners, it would be too tricky. Making loose covers for sofas and armchairs involves wrestling large amounts of fabric through the sewing machine, so I recommend that beginners find a professional to make any loose covers for them. This little number is not difficult to construct, however, and the pink velvet buttons are easy to make with the help of a covered-button kit.

MATERIALS

the following makes a cover for a small upholstered chair

210cm cotton calico,
   at least 112cm wide
scrap of velvet for covering
   buttons
kit for making 9 fabric-covered
   buttons 3cm in diameter
sewing thread

E BACK (CHAIR BACK) CUT 1	**B** CHAIR SEAT CUT 1	**A** FRONT (CHAIR BACK) CUT 1

C SKIRT
CUT 1

D SIDES
CUT 1

1 SQUARE = 10CM

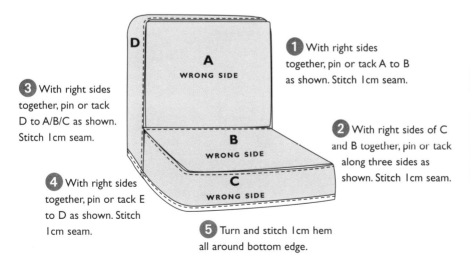

3 With right sides together, pin or tack D to A/B/C as shown. Stitch 1cm seam.

4 With right sides together, pin or tack E to D as shown. Stitch 1cm seam.

1 With right sides together, pin or tack A to B as shown. Stitch 1cm seam.

2 With right sides of C and B together, pin or tack along three sides as shown. Stitch 1cm seam.

5 Turn and stitch 1cm hem all around bottom edge.

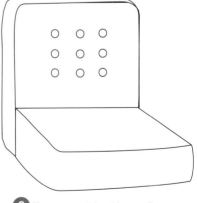

6 Turn cover right side out. Press. Cover nine buttons with velvet. Sew buttons to chair back in square shape as shown.

towelling and gingham stool cover

Most bathrooms are a little on the small side so a bathside stool that you can plonk anything on from the baby's bottom, the radio, or that well-deserved glass of champagne comes in most handy. Make a soft towelling cushion cover with a simple envelope back, so it's easily removeable for washing, and if you require extra security, attach ribbons underneath to it tie in place.

MATERIALS

the following makes one cushion measuring 28cm by 18cm

110cm cotton towelling, at least 50cm wide
30cm cotton gingham, 112cm wide, for frill
sewing thread
wadding, 60cm by 40cm and 2.5cm thick

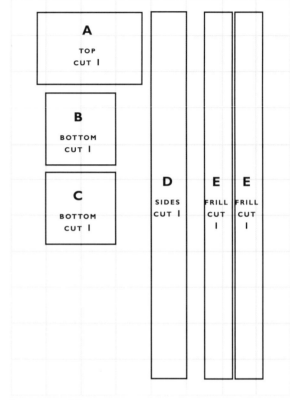

I SQUARE = 10CM

1 With right sides together, pin or tack D to A. Stitch 1cm seam.

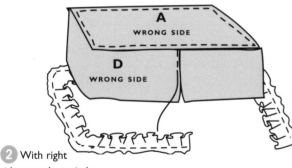

2 With right sides together, stitch narrow ends of E together with 1cm seam to make a continuous strip. Turn and stitch 1cm hem on E. Gather frill E to fit all the way around D (see Simple Sewing Techniques on page 13).

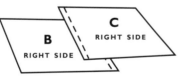

3 Turn and stitch 1cm hem on one long side of B and C. Press.

4 Pin or tack B and C to bottom edge of D with hemmed edges overlapping in the centre and frill E sandwiched in between as shown. Stitch 1cm seam all the way around.

5 With right sides together, stitch short ends of D with 1cm seam. Press.

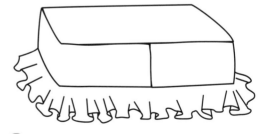

6 Stitch ends of frill together with 1cm seam. Turn cover right side out. Press. Cut 2 layers of wadding, each 1cm less all the way round than the stitched piece A. (You may need to add further layers of wadding to gain enough thickness.) Fill cover with wadding.

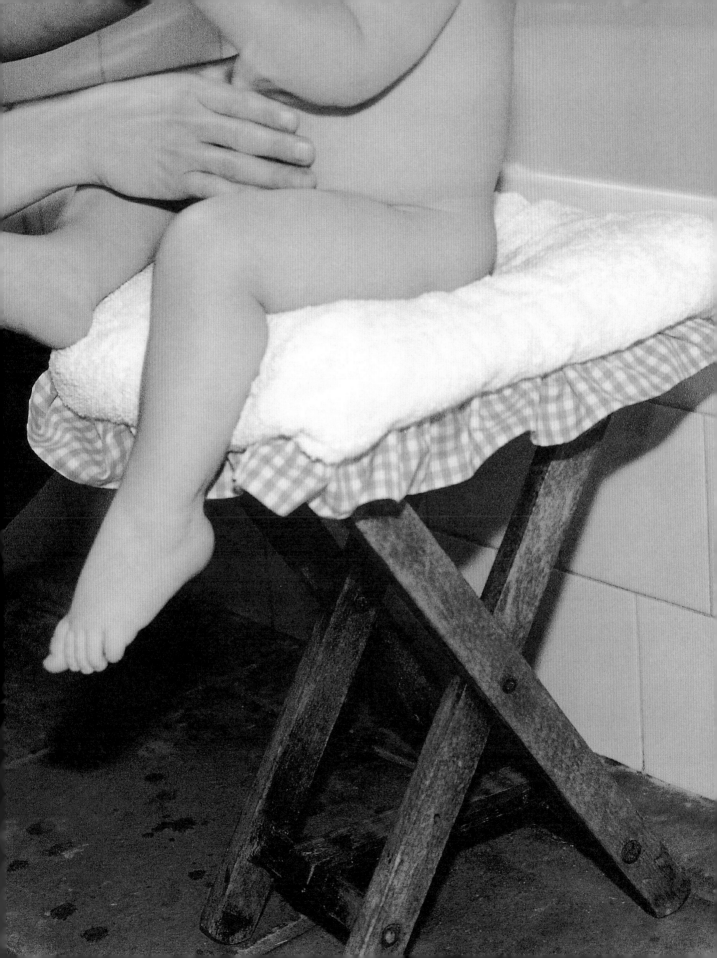

revamped armchair cover

If your favourite loose chair cover has seen better days or you're simply bored with its looks, ring the changes by stitching on patches in contrasting prints or even adding a frill. Here a blue ticking chair cover has acquired a pioneer-cowgirl look with patches and frills in a tiny 'home-on-the-range' rosebud print. Check patterned chair covers could also benefit from the same treatment if combined with something pretty and floral.

MATERIALS
odd pieces of fabric from
your remnants bag
sewing thread

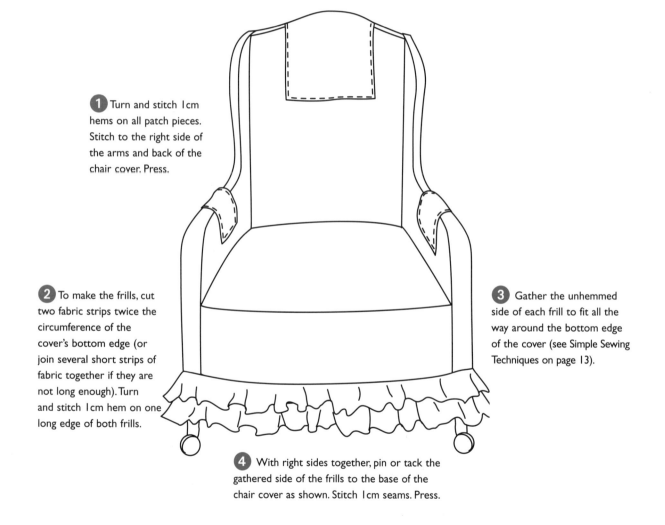

1 Turn and stitch 1cm hems on all patch pieces. Stitch to the right side of the arms and back of the chair cover. Press.

2 To make the frills, cut two fabric strips twice the circumference of the cover's bottom edge (or join several short strips of fabric together if they are not long enough). Turn and stitch 1cm hem on one long edge of both frills.

3 Gather the unhemmed side of each frill to fit all the way around the bottom edge of the cover (see Simple Sewing Techniques on page 13).

4 With right sides together, pin or tack the gathered side of the frills to the base of the chair cover as shown. Stitch 1cm seams. Press.

smart ideas for chairs

ten tips for bargain buys

1 Don't pull up right outside the shop in your Mercedes convertible. Park out of sight or take the bus.

2 Dress down for your shopping expedition. Some sellers may up the price if they think you're rolling in it, so leave off your diamonds.

3 Look around the shop or stall and focus your interest on a piece that you don't want. Make some bogus enquiries into what you aren't interested in, then nonchalantly ask the price of the chair you really have your eye on. This way you won't reveal your burning desire to have it, which will only encourage the trader to put the price up.

4 If there are two chairs and you want them both, ask for a discount. The seller may be keen to sell them as a pair, rather than be left with an odd one.

5 Offer cash rather than a cheque or a credit card. That way, you're more likely to get a discount.

6 Don't get carried away and offer more than you can afford. Walk away if you can't get your price, or at least agree half-way.

7 Don't go to obviously trendy stalls at markets. I have found my best buys in anonymous high streets where no one knows or cares whether your purchase is a Bertoia or vintage Ercol.

8 Salerooms with regular auctions can be another source of great buys. Check local papers for details of one near you.

9 Check all furniture for woodworm – tiny pinholes. It's treatable but may have damaged a piece so badly that it could collapse on you.

10 Test joints by pushing from the back. Check chair legs to see if they have been repaired. Don't buy a piece if they have.

DRESSING UP CHAIRS

A flirty, frilly cover can transform a plain Jane into a sexy Susan (a chair that is) with just the minimum of time and angst spent over the sewing machine. I discovered this and other simple sartorial effects whilst renovating our old Georgian terrace house in Spitalfields, East London on a shoestring. Most of our funds were swallowed up by enormous building costs – the back wall and roof had to be completely rebuilt – so there was very little left over for fabrics and other decorating materials, in other words, all the fun bits.

Inspired by the rules of good housekeeping, strictly adhered to by the owners of old-fashioned English country houses who shroud their expensively upholstered furniture in dust sheets when leaving their stately piles for a season on the Cote d'Azur or skiing in Gstaad, I recently went in search of cheap calico to do the same thing, albeit on a more modest scale. Rather than protection from dust and moths, my covers were a quick and stylish fabric facelift for a motley assortment of battered and not-so-battered chairs accumulated over the years. Parked in a corner amongst unpainted woodwork and debris of house rennovations, my sewing machine humming in unison with the whine of the builder's power tools, I devised a number of covers for use all around the house: a bathroom chair in white linen, kitchen chairs with durable pull-on covers in thick cotton and bedroom chairs with ties and frilly skirts in ticking and gingham.

CHOOSING CHAIRS TO COVER

I've stuck to ideas for smallish chairs, and haven't included a loose cover for big armchair as they are not that easy to tackle. It would be easier to ask a pro to make a bigger loose cover with arms, and other awkard shapes, until you are more comfortable handling and sewing larger quantities of fabric.

UNIFY mis-matching shapes and styles of chairs with sets of plain cream covers. This is a great way of creating a stylish dinner table. Wooden kitchen chairs are usually good value and can be made more comfortable with a squab seat.

GIVE a similar treatment to standard stacking school chairs and old factory seating (see the Flower Power Chair Cover on pages 46–7). Pick them up from junk shops or at markets.

USE a basic folding director's chair either indoors or outdoors for a cheap seating solution.

EMBELLISH a classic design, such as the folding deckchair, with your own additions (see the Deckchair Pillow on pages 44–5). There are also numerous takes on striped deckchair canvas, so you can choose your favourite colourway.

SEEK out some of the numerous places specialising in redundant office furniture and equipment. Swivel office chairs are also good for updating (see the Groovy Office Chair Cover on pages 52–3). On a practical note, the more time you spend sitting, the more adjustable your chair should be. And a chair like this with adjustable height can be used by everyone in the family.

HANDY HINTS FOR WASHING CHAIR COVERS

DRY CLEAN heavy fabrics such as velvet for the best results.

TEST all coloured fabrics for colour fastness. If the dye is loose, either dry clean or hand wash quickly in warm water.

PREWASH fabrics before stitching to pre-shrink. If a finished cover does shrink and is difficult to fit, rinse in warm water and hang out to dry. While the cover is still fairly damp, gently stretch on to the chair. Once the cover is in position, press with a moderate iron.

PAINTING A JUNK CHAIR

My favourite colours for sprucing up old chairs are duck-egg blues or plain whites. First sand the chair with a medium grain sandpaper, and then again with a fine sandpaper. Be sure to remove any loose bits of old varnish or flakes of old paint to leave a perfectly smooth surface. Once sanded, wipe off all dust before painting. Apply one coat of wood primer or undercoat as evenly as possible. Allow to dry thoroughly. Apply one layer of eggshell paint. Allow to dry thoroughly before applying a second coat of paint.

ten ideas for fabrics

1 Most fabrics are suitable for covering chairs. Since only small amounts are required, you could splash out on something more expensive.

2 Adding a chair cover is a really good way of introducing splashes of bright colour into a room.

3 Then, of course, there are cotton tickings, plain calico and linen, all of which are great textures for simple chair covers.

4 Even towelling should be considered (see the Towelling and Gingham Stool Cover on pages 58–9), as it obviously works well in bathrooms and also comes in good blues and plain white.

5 When trying to do things cheaply, the trick is to think laterally and see what you can do with less obvious ideas (see the Linen Tea Towel Chair Cover on pages 48–9 where a chair has been given a new lease of life with, of all things, an ordinary blue and white linen tea towel).

6 Creamy coloured calico in the heaviest weight you can find is both cheap and durable.

7 If you're bothered by the creasing of linen – personally I don't mind – then don't use it for dining chairs that endure wear and tear and also need to be washed and ironed regularly.

8 Hessian is suitable for covering chairs used in the garden. Again, it's very cheap and cheerful.

9 Muslin is too thin to be seriously considered as a robust chair cover but can be used to make a romantic see-through shape for a pretty bedroom chair.

10 Linen roller towelling can be difficult to obtain, but only the other day I saw some cheap lengths at a stall selling ex-hotel and hospital linens in my local street market. It's worth looking out for.

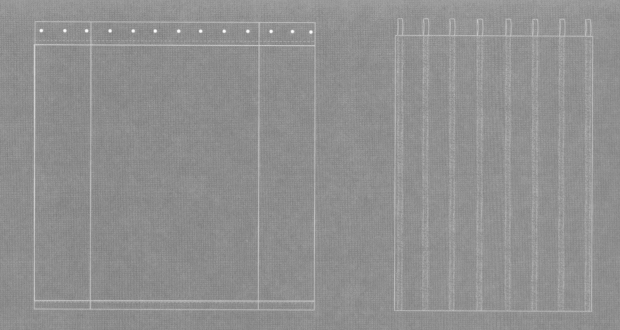

ten essential curtains

HAVE A GO AT RUNNING UP THESE SIMPLE IDEAS FOR WINDOW TREATMENTS – A BASIC ROLL-UP LINEN BLIND, PERHAPS, OR A PLAIN MUSLIN PANEL – AND SCREENING – A PATCHWORK CURTAIN TO HIDE HOUSEHOLD STORAGE OR A SHADY STRIPED CANVAS AWNING OUTSIDE FOR A LONG SUNDAY LUNCH OUTSIDE. NONE WILL HAVE YOU FRETTING OVER THE SEWING MACHINE AND THERE ARE NO COMPLICATED PELMETS, LININGS, OR FIDDLY HEADINGS TO WORRY ABOUT.

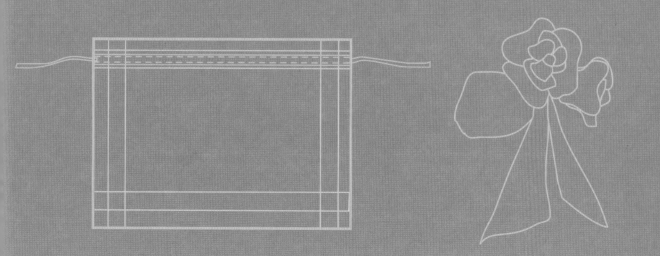

roller blind with scallops

When we moved into our last flat with its large warehouse-style windows I took the line of least resistance and ordered thirteen plain white roller blinds from a department store, fitting included. However, when we finally move into our new home, I have promised to make blinds for our girls and might suggest something like this gingham roller blind made with a scalloped trim. Instead of the scallop detail I might attach a contrasting band stitched with layers of rick-rack and ribbon (see the Stripey Rick-rack Tablecloth on pages 94–5).

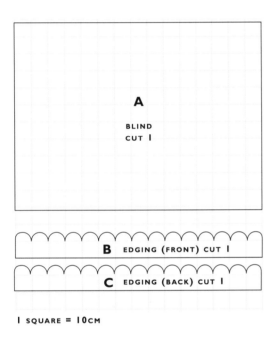

1 SQUARE = 10CM

MATERIALS

the following makes a blind 150cm wide by 113cm long, including the edging

130cm gingham cotton, 150cm wide
160cm linen, at least 40cm wide
roller blind kit (available from department stores)
sewing thread

1 With right sides together, pin or tack B to C. Stitch 1cm seam along sides and scalloped edges as shown.

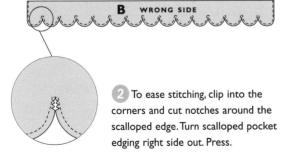

2 To ease stitching, clip into the corners and cut notches around the scalloped edge. Turn scalloped pocket edging right side out. Press.

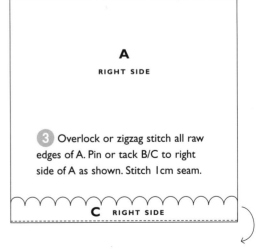

3 Overlock or zigzag stitch all raw edges of A. Pin or tack B/C to right side of A as shown. Stitch 1cm seam.

4 Fold down scalloped edge and press. Now make up the roller blind with the scalloped edge according to the kit instructions.

ruffle curtain

If you are a streamlined minimalist, stop right here. Isn't it about time you introduced a little ruffly glamour into your life? With stitched-on lengths of gathered lightweight polyester that has been ripped rather than cut, this filmy curtain would look stunning floating at a large loft window. Hang the looped heading from a pole or stretched wire. It will even survive a low-temperature wash and short spin.

MATERIALS

the following makes ruffles for a ready-made curtain 180cm wide by 250cm long

shop-bought cotton curtain with
   a looped heading, measuring
   180cm wide by 250cm long
220cm polyester, at least 90cm wide
sewing thread

1 Make eight long strips by stitching two strips A together end to end. Leaving the edges raw, gather each strip along the centre to fit the full length of the curtain as shown (see Simple Sewing Techniques on page 13).

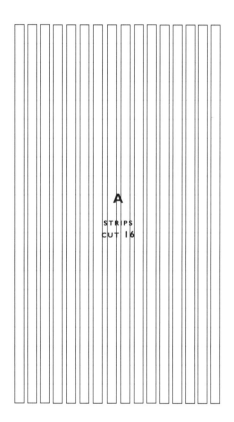

A

STRIPS
CUT 16

I SQUARE = 10CM

2 Pin or tack the gathered strips to the curtain at regular intervals as shown. Stitch each strip down the centre to secure.

flowery curtain tie-back

Make a curtain tie-back with a more striking modern look than those fuddy-duddy tassels loved by the English country-house brigade. Fake flowers – the blousier the better – pinned on to a band of checked fabric is a great idea for a girlie boudoir. Likewise, try plain bands of white organza tied in a big bow for an equally romantic effect. One of the simplest tie-back ideas is lengths of ribbon tied and looped on a hook attached to the windowframe or adjoining wall.

MATERIALS

the following makes one tie-back measuring 10cm by 118cm

40cm gingham cotton, at least 137cm wide
sewing thread
3 silk flowers
safety pin

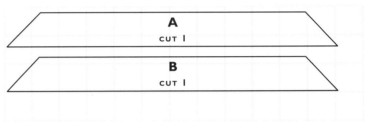

I SQUARE = 10CM

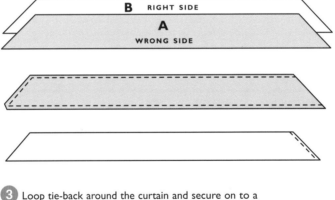

1 With right sides together, pin or tack A to B. Stitch 1cm seam around three sides as shown. Clip off point at corner as shown. Turn tie-back right side out. Press.

2 Fold 1cm to the inside around the opening and pin or tack. Stitch the opening close to the edge to secure.

3 Loop tie-back around the curtain and secure on to a hook with a bow or a knot.

4 Attach silk flowers to the centre of the tie-back, using a safety pin.

stripey canvas awning

One of the best things about the summer holidays are the long, languid lunches shared with friends gossiping and being greedy. I love eating al fresco, and to keep everyone cool, I make a shady awning from a tough canvas – the darker the colour the better to stop the sun's rays from penetrating – to stretch across a metal frame put up outside. If you want to be able to whisk the awning away quickly, tie the loops to your frame.

MATERIALS

the following makes an awning approximately 300cm by 194cm

300cm by 200cm piece of striped canvas (available from hardware shops)
7.5m cotton tape, 2.5cm wide
sewing thread

1 Turn over 4cm hem on both raw edges of the piece of canvas and pin or tack. Stitch hem 2cm from edge.

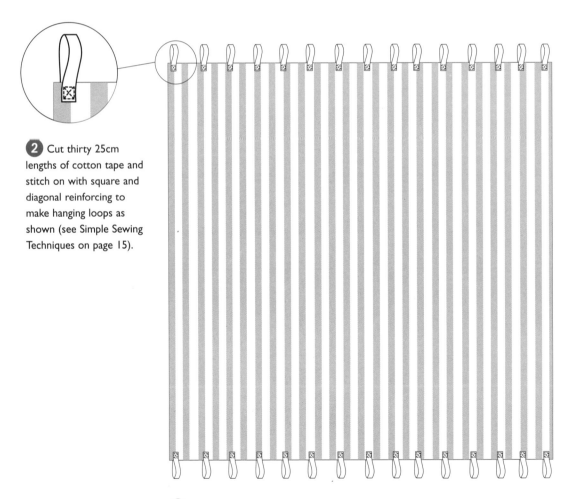

2 Cut thirty 25cm lengths of cotton tape and stitch on with square and diagonal reinforcing to make hanging loops as shown (see Simple Sewing Techniques on page 15).

3 Slip the loops on to the frame or tie them on with ribbon or rope.

patchwork alcove curtain

If you have the sizeable budget carpentry requires, the neatest storage solution in a room with alcoves is to build floor-to-ceiling shelves. If funds are tight, however, and you can not face the prospect of gazing at shelves laden with clutter, head for your workbag of remnants to stitch a homespun patchwork curtain. Use old denim cutoffs, pale blue stripes and fifties florals. To hang the curtain, make plain loops to slide across a pole fitted from edge to edge of the alcove. This idea works equally well for curtaining off an unsightly office area at home or at work.

MATERIALS
the following makes one curtain measuring 115cm wide by 148cm long

enough remnants from your workbag to make a curtain measuring 115cm by 148cm
sewing thread

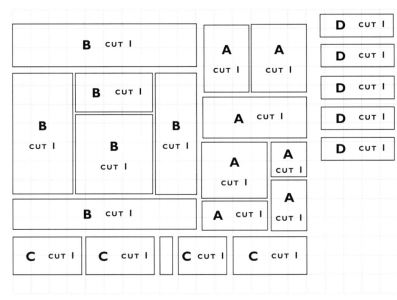

I SQUARE = 10CM

* As this is a patchwork, remember that the pieces will be cut from varying fabrics

1 Stitch together A, B and C as separate blocks of patchwork, with 1cm seams. Press open seams as you proceed. Join block A to block B, then A/B to C, with 1cm seams, to make one piece. Press.

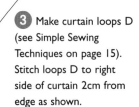

2 Turn and stitch 1cm hem along both long sides of curtain.

3 Make curtain loops D (see Simple Sewing Techniques on page 15). Stitch loops D to right side of curtain 2cm from edge as shown.

4 Fold loops away from curtain and press 2cm hem along top. Stitch hem 1cm from top edge. Turn and stitch 1cm hem at bottom edge.

plastic and towelling shower curtain

When a walk-in wet room just isn't an option, then that good old bathroom standby, the plastic shower curtain, is a useful but not very interesting device, particularly when spattered with soap stains and spots of mould. So it was a stroke of good luck when I came across some end-of-the-line, fifties-style roller towels, normally destined for some institutional washroom or other, in my favourite haberdashery shop. I decided that they'd look smart sewn into a stylish retro curtain, which could be attached to a plastic waterproof lining and hung in the shower.

1 With right sides of selvedges together, pin or tack the lengths of roller towel to either side of the towelling panel. Stitch 5mm seams. (There's no need to hem the outer edges as they have selvedges.)

2 Turn and stitch 6cm hem at top of curtain.

3 Line up towelling curtain with plastic curtain. Mark the position of the eyelets on the towelling curtain. Using the hole-punching kit, punch eyelets in the towelling curtain.

4 Turn and stitch 1cm hem on bottom edge of curtain.

5 Thread 30cm lengths of ribbon through eyelets of both curtains. Tie on to shower curtain pole.

MATERIALS

the following makes a towelling curtain 178cm wide by 183cm long

plastic shower curtain, 177cm by 177cm, for lining
2 linen roller towels, 190cm by 40cm
190cm cotton towelling, 100cm wide
eyelet kit with 13 eyelets (or same number as plastic curtain)
4m ribbon, 2cm wide
sewing thread

roll-up linen blind

A lightweight linen blind that rolls up easily is the ideal window treatment for a simple beach hut, a small terrace house or a cottage with low windows. Unless you are happy to grapple with metres of fabric and a stepladder, I wouldn't recommend this blind for very large windows or those that are situated high up a wall. The ties could be simplified even further by using wide widths of cotton tape or ribbon cut to length.

MATERIALS
the following makes a blind
120cm wide by 143cm long

170cm linen, 120cm wide
130cm cotton, at least 90cm wide
sewing thread
eyelet kit with 4 eyelets
4 cup hooks

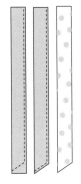

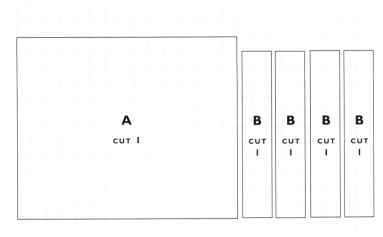

A
CUT 1

B
CUT 1

B
CUT 1

B
CUT 1

B
CUT 1

1 SQUARE = 10CM

1 Make four ties B (see Simple Sewing Techniques on page 13).

2 For the hem at the top of A (one of raw edges), turn and press 1cm then 5cm to wrong side and pin. Insert ties under hem and pin or tack. Stitch hem across the width of the blind. (There's no need to hem the sides of blind as they have selvedges.)

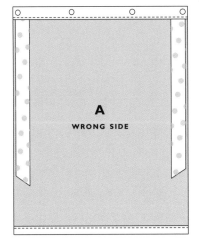

A
WRONG SIDE

3 Stitch ties D to right side of A to correspond with those on wrong side.

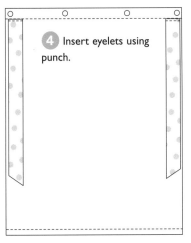

4 Insert eyelets using punch.

5 Turn and stitch 1cm hem at bottom edge of blind. Hang blind from cup hooks.

thick corduroy curtain

As part of our national obsession with the weather, the English hate being chilly (completely understandable, I'd say). In my childhood – before the days of central heating – the adults used up a lot of energy shouting at us to 'shut that door, you're letting in a draught.' Most houses are riddled with breezy nooks and crannies, so if your pad is chilly, think about installing a thick draught-excluding curtain lined with a blanket on a rod across the front door – a chief entry point for the dreaded draughts. It will go a long way to keeping your home toasty.

MATERIALS

the following makes one curtain measuring 148cm wide by 199cm long:

260cm cotton corduroy, 150cm wide woollen blanket cut to 198cm by 146cm
scraps of contrasting fabric for
   contrasitng loops (optional)
sewing thread

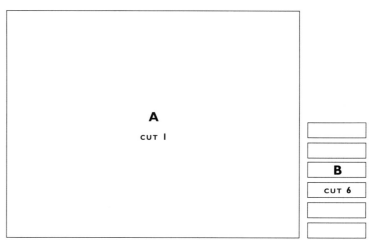

A

CUT 1

B

CUT 6

I SQUARE = 10CM

1 Cut the blanket to size leaving the blanket-stitched edge at the top intact. There's no need to hem the sides as felted wool will not fray.

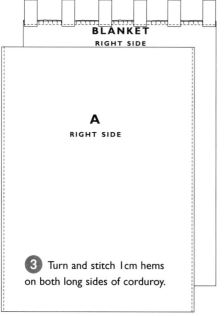

BLANKET
RIGHT SIDE

A
RIGHT SIDE

3 Turn and stitch 1cm hems on both long sides of corduroy.

2 From corduroy (or contrasting fabric), make six loops B (see Simple Sewing Techniques on page 13) and stitch to top of blanket at regular intervals as shown.

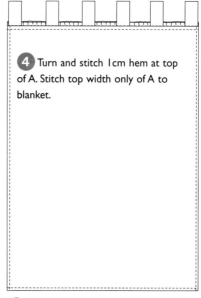

4 Turn and stitch 1cm hem at top of A. Stitch top width only of A to blanket.

5 Turn and stitch 1cm hem along bottom edge of A.

muslin window panel

There might be architect-designed state-of-the-art ideas to prevent curious passers-by from having a good nose through your windows, but I have found that there isn't anything simpler or cheaper than muslin. Fix up panels of muslin edged with tape and tied on to hooks at all four corners of your windows.

MATERIALS

the following makes one curtain panel measuring 88cm by 88cm:

100cm muslin, 100cm wide
5m cotton tape, 1.5cm wide
sewing thread
4 cup hooks

1 Overlock or zigzag stitch all raw edges of A. Turn and stitch 1cm hem all the wary around.

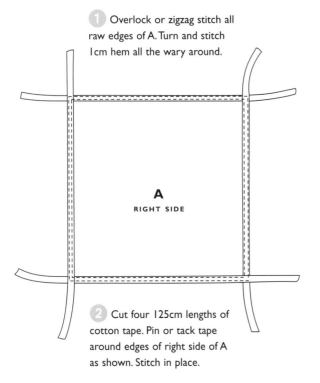

A

RIGHT SIDE

2 Cut four 125cm lengths of cotton tape. Pin or tack tape around edges of right side of A as shown. Stitch in place.

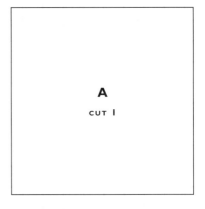

A

CUT 1

1 SQUARE = 10CM

3 Tie panel on to cup hooks screwed into window frame.

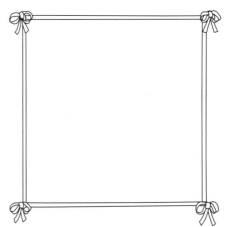

handy tea towel drape

My favourite tea towel is here again as a sweet alternative to a dingy bit of net curtaining. No need to bother with hemming any edges as they're already finished – all that's required is some cotton bias binding to make a casing for the ribbon that will secure the curtain and allow it to be lightly gathered. This idea is particularly good in bathrooms where it is preferable to have an opaque texture rather than something more transparent like muslin, which will silhouette the occupant rather more than might be desired.

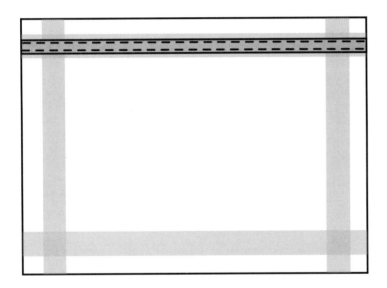

 Pin or tack the bias binding to the tea towel 3cm from the top edge as shown, turning under ends. Stitch close to the edge along both long sides of binding, leaving the ends open.

MATERIALS
the following makes one curtain measuring 65cm wide by 48cm long

cotton tea towel measuring 65cm by 48cm
sewing thread
70cm bias binding, 2.5cm wide
2 screw-in hooks
1.1m ribbon, 12mm wide
safety pin

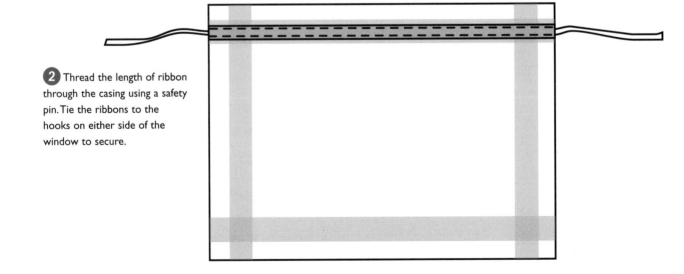

2 Thread the length of ribbon through the casing using a safety pin. Tie the ribbons to the hooks on either side of the window to secure.

smart ideas for windows

ten tips for windows

1 Choose a warm but dull day for window cleaning. Frost, rain or sun will make the job difficult.

2 There are many proprietary window cleaners, but the best and quickest method is the window-cleaner's way: a damp chamois leather and a dry piece of linen scrim. It is essential the leather is a good one, large enough and very clean.

3 Add a squeeze of washing-up liquid to hot water if your windows are really dirty, but never use soap powders or the chamois leather will become slimy and the windows smeary.

4 My granny used paraffin as a cleaner for windows and mirrors. Apply with an old cloth and then polish off with absorbent kitchen paper.

5 Crumpled newspaper is another old-fashioned window cleaning tool.

6 For streak-free windows, add a few drops of vinegar to the cleaning water.

7 When washing window frames, you can use a proprietary paint cleaner but ordinary washing-up liquid can be just as efficient. Have a bowl of hot soapy water and one of clean warm water for rinsing. Use a sponge or absorbent cloth.

8 Revive filthy window frames – especially in kitchens and bathrooms which become dull and shabby due to steam, condensation and grease – by rubbing briskly with a clean cloth dripped in linseed oil. Leave for a while then polish off with a warm, soft duster.

9 Obstinate marks on paintwork can be removed by rubbing very gently with fine steel wool dipped in turpentine.

10 Window sash cords will last longer and work more efficiently if they are rubbed with hard soap. This treatment can also be given to blind cords.

FIRST AID FOR EVERYDAY SPOTS AND STAINS

It's not worth getting stressed over spots and stains; simply face the fact that wear and tear is part of everyday living. Ideally, treat any stain the moment it occurs. Once a stain has penetrated the fibres of fabric it is more difficult to dislodge, but while it is still on the surface quick simple cleaning will usually remove it. Immediate measures include rinsing non-greasy stains with plain cold water and dusting grease spots with talcum powder. With fabrics that are not normally washable, begin with the simplest methods first. Very often sponging with clear, warm water will be sufficient to remove a fresh, non-greasy stain. Only resort to chemicals when all other methods have failed.

Remove stains before laundering as washing may make them permanent. Most stains, especially thick or greasy marks, should be treated from the wrong side of the material so that the stains are pushed out on to a clean pad underneath. If cleaning is started from the right side of the fabric the dirt must be pushed right through before it can be completely removed. If using stain-removing liquids, test on an inconspicuous part of the fabric such as an inside seam before treating, particularly with delicate or coloured fabrics. Rinse all stain removers thoroughly as they may weaken the fibres.

Whether you live in a grimy city or out in the countryside, curtains and blinds suffer extra wear and tear wherever there are children, pets, lots of partying and in kitchens, bathroom and doorways leading outside. Here are some simple remedies for common stain culprits.

BALLPOINT PEN stains should be sponged with methylated spirit and rinsed.

CANDLE WAX should be scraped away as much as possible if blown on to a nearby curtain. Then place a sheet of blotting paper under the stain and another on top and press lightly with a warm iron. Where the wax is very difficult to remove, an ice cube held against the wax often helps.

CHEWING GUM has been know to have been stuck to curtains by small people trying to hide the evidence. On washable fabrics apply a little egg white and when the gum is soft pick off as much as possible and launder in the usual way. Or rub the gum with ice, pick off the loose pieces and wash.

CHOCOLATE can be sponged off with a warm borax solution of 30g borax to 500ml water. Rinse and launder in the usual way.

GREASE AND OIL can be removed by sprinkling over talcum powder or fuller's earth. Spread the powder over the stain and replace as it becomes saturated. Leave for several hours before brushing off.

JAM stains should be washed immediately in hot detergent suds. However, if the stain has dried into the material and persists after washing, soak in 500ml warm water with 30g borax. Leave for 20 minutes then rinse thoroughly and wash in warm soapy water.

MILDEW stains can appear on summer curtains and awnings that have been packed away over a wet humid winter. Ordinary laundering should remove mildew stains while they are still fresh enough for the growth to be on the fabric surface. It sounds pretty unpalatable, but soaking in sour milk and leaving in the sun to dry is often effective if repeated several times. Moistening with lemon juice and salt and drying in the sun may also help. Old mildew stains can sometimes be removed from white cottons and linens with diluted household bleach.

MUD should not be removed while wet. Allow the stain to dry thoroughly, then remove gently with a stiff brush. For washable fabrics, launder in the usual way.

WATER spotting can be a problem in bathrooms. Try holding the material in the steam from a boiling kettle until the fabric is damp. Shake often while steaming, then press with a warm iron while still damp.

WINE stains should be treated immediately whenever possible. Dissolve 30g borax in 350ml hot water and either soak the stained area in the solution or sponge it on to the fabric. Leave for half and hour, then wash in warm soapy water and rinse thoroughly. By the way, pouring salt on red wine is the worst possible thing you can do, according to experts.

MEASURING UP FOR CURTAINS

When buying fabric for a pair of curtains, allow one-and-a-half to one-and-three-quarters times the width of the window for each curtain. Allow approximately 15cm more than the desired finished curtain length for the hems. If the curtain is to reach to the ground, err on the long rather the short side – curtains that are too short look like short trousers on an overgrown schoolboy.

ten tips for curtain care

1 Test all fabrics for colour fastness before laundering. If the dye is loose, wash quickly in warm suds. Rinse in warm water and dry as speedily as possible.

2 Check all curtain fabrics have been pre-shrunk before washing or you may have a nasty surprise when re-hanging.

3 Most cotton will stand fairly hard treatment. Whites are most efficiently laundered in a washing-machine at 85°C.

4 Most unlined curtains can be washed at home, but anything lined and in a heavy furnishing fabric such as velvet are better dry-cleaned professionally.

5 Launder light curtains frequently. Take them down from the windows, remove all hooks or rings and shake well or brush with the vacuum cleaner to remove dust.

6 Grubby curtains should be soaked overnight in warm water with gentle detergent, and then washed in the usual way the next morning.

7 Wash muslin curtains in warm water and rinse several times before wringing out. Pin each corner to a sheet or old tablecloth before hanging to dry. Iron while still damp, going around the edges to set the shape.

8 Plastic curtains can be washed in warm suds and rinsed in clear warm water. Don't rub, wring or twist the curtains, wipe off surplus moisture with a towel and hang to dry and then rub with a clean cloth and re-hang.

9 Roller blinds made from coated cottons can be sponged down with water and a little washing-up liquid if need to remove grime and stains.

10 Iron freshly laundered curtains while still slightly damp. Iron on the wrong side of the fabric to avoid any shine.

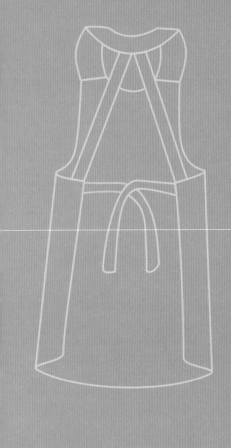

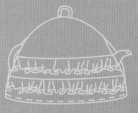

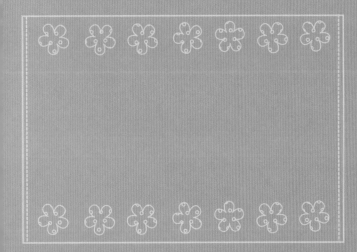

ten essential table linens

WHETHER YOU'RE PACKING UP A PICNIC FOR THE BEACH OR HAVING TEA FOR TWO, IT DOESN'T REQUIRE MUCH FUSS AND BOTHER TO MAKE A CRISP TABLECLOTH EMBELLISHED WITH A RIBBON TRIM OR NAPKINS FROM LINENS IN BRIGHT SUGARED ALMOND PINKS AND GREENS. THERE'S EVEN A SEXY POLKA DOT APRON FOR LOOKING CUTE WHEN YOU'RE DOING THE WASHING UP.

chambray ruffle tablecloth

Chambray is the lightweight cousin of denim and is another all-purpose cotton that has an honest workaday appearance, which improves with washing as it fades and softens. It is a very good choice for table linen if only for the fact that its sludgy blue colour will weather stains more readily than a crisp white linen. A plain edged chambray cloth looks smart, but I thought that adding a frill would give it a 'home-on-the-range' feel that would look good in anything from an urban flat to a cottage in the country. You could also run up some napkins to match.

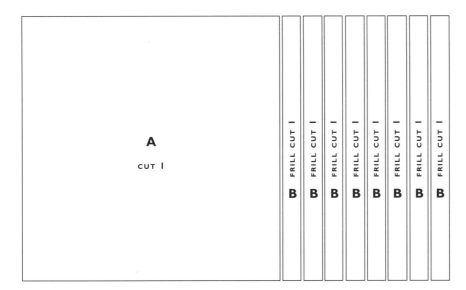

A
CUT 1

FRILL CUT 1 B | FRILL CUT 1 B | FRILL CUT 1 B | FRILL CUT 1 B | FRILL CUT 1 B | FRILL CUT 1 B | FRILL CUT 1 B | FRILL CUT 1 B

1 SQUARE = 10CM

MATERIALS

the following makes a tablecloth measuring 144cm by 144cm, including frill

270cm cotton chambray denim, at least 137cm wide

sewing thread

1 With right sides together, stitch narrow ends of B together with 1cm seams to make one continuous strip. Press seams open. For frill hem, turn and press 1cm then 2cm to wrong side along one long side and pin or tack. Stitch in place. Gather unhemmed edge of frill B to fit all the way around A (see Simple Sewing Techniques on page 13).

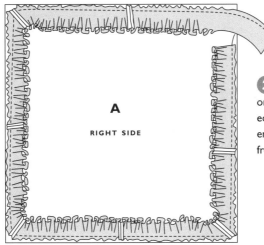

A
RIGHT SIDE

2 With right sides together, pin or tack gathered edge of frill B to edges of A. Stitch 1cm seam. Stitch ends of frill together. Press frill away from centre of tablecloth.

simple stitched table runner

Remember primary school and those first faltering hand-stitched attempts on little pieces of craft fabric. Well here's your chance to re-live the experience. I have to say that even the most practically challenged individual would be able to embellish this simple linen table runner. All you need is a needle with a big eye – no problems for threading here – and some cotton yarn (pure wool will not survive high temperatures in the washing machine) in colours that you like. If sewing in a straight line is potentially awkward, mark out the line very faintly in dressmaker's chalk.

MATERIALS
linen runner, measuring 190cm
   by 40cm
dressmaker's chalk
large-eyed needle
cotton yarn

1 Using some dressmaker's chalk, mark out 2 bands of stitches around the edge of the right side of the linen runner.

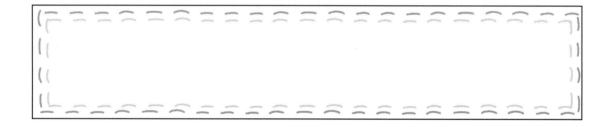

2 Using a needle with a large eye, work running stitch where marked by the chalk.

stripey rick-rack tablecloth

For a thrifty take on the 'Little-House-on-the-Prairie' look – denims, hominy grits, clapboard houses and all that homesteading flavour – trim the end widths of an old sheet or piece of white cotton with ribbon and rick-rack. Just pin and sew on strips of plain rick-rack and bias binding, or sew the rick-rack on to ribbon for contrast. Stick to a blue-and-white colour theme, as I have here, or try something more riotous in a mixture of pinks, greens and hot oranges. This makes a great summer picnic cloth.

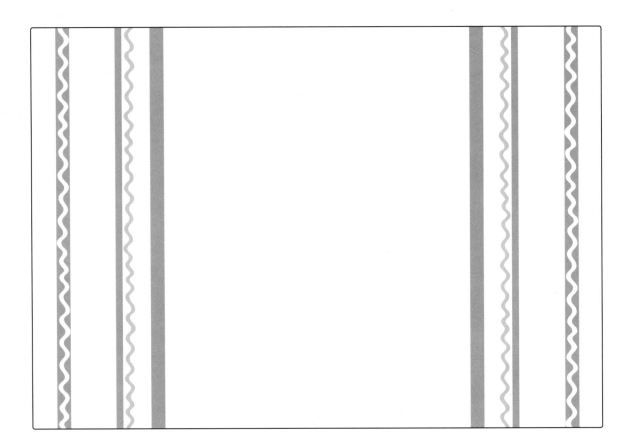

1 Cut lengths of rick-rack and bias binding to fit the width of the tablecloth. Pin or tack in place, keeping the bias binding flat. Stitch in place, sewing as close to the edges of the bias binding and ribbon as possible but down the centre of the rick-rack. Turn and stitch 1cm hem all around edge.

MATERIALS
the following makes one tablecloth measuring 138cm by 98cm:

140cm medium-weight cotton, 100cm wide, or an old tablecloth or bedsheet trimmed to this size
1m lengths each of ribbon, rick-rack and bias binding
sewing thread

coloured linen napkins

There's something unarguably understated and fresh about crisply ironed white linens, and I'm the first to write at great length on the simplicity and stylishness of the white table setting. However, my love of simple white linens doesn't preclude a passion for splashes of brilliant bright colour – the fuchsia pink lips are mine – at the table in the form of a gorgeous scented hyacinth, or a pile of Neapolitan ice-cream coloured linen napkins like these. Intermittent colour doesn't detract from food, particularly if it is served on plain white plates.

1 Stitch the bias binding around the edge of the fabric (see Simple Sewing Techniques on page 15).

MATERIALS
the following makes one napkin
measuring 50cm by 50cm

50cm by 50cm piece of dress
    linen for each napkin
2.2m bias binding, 2cm wide, for
    each napkin
sewing thread

polka-dot pinny

At the risk of offending ardent feminists who see them as a symbol of female servility, I think that the apron is an indispensable item of work wear. What better way to protect your little Prada number from children's teatime before the babysitter arrives? If you want to cut a certain domestic dash, there is nothing offensive about a traditional crisp white chef's apron or a simple utilitarian blue-and-white striped butcher's pinny, but for something a little more sweet and sexy when brandishing the vacuum cleaner, the polka-dot pinny here is based on a traditional forties style that ties rather fetchingly at the back.

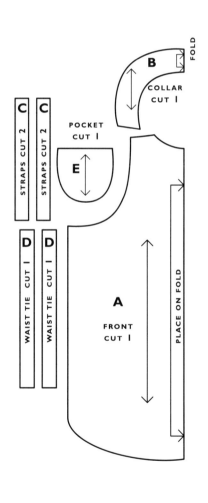

I SQUARE = 10CM

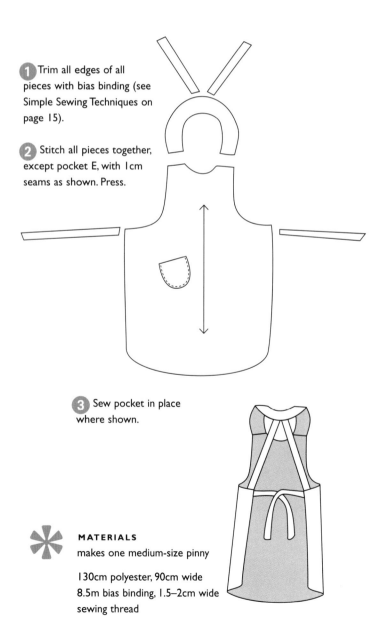

1 Trim all edges of all pieces with bias binding (see Simple Sewing Techniques on page 15).

2 Stitch all pieces together, except pocket E, with 1cm seams as shown. Press.

3 Sew pocket in place where shown.

MATERIALS
makes one medium-size pinny

130cm polyester, 90cm wide
8.5m bias binding, 1.5–2cm wide
sewing thread

appliqué daisy tablecloth

More commonly found in the garden shed, hessian has a utilitarian no-nonsense appeal that makes its elevation from humble sacking to rustic interior chic unsurprising – it's currently all the rage for walls, floors and cushions. I bought a bundle of hessian from my favourite fabric wholesaler with this resilient outdoor tablecloth in mind. The groovy sixties-style appliquéd daisies are a quick way to add some colourful decoration.

I SQUARE = 10CM

✳ MATERIALS

the following makes a tablecloth measuring 192cm by 150cm

200cm hessian, 150cm wide
100cm polyester, at least 70cm wide
100cm iron-on interfacing, at least 70cm wide
card for template
sewing thread

1 To hem hessian at each end, turn and press 1cm then 3cm to wrong side and pin or tack. Stitch in place.

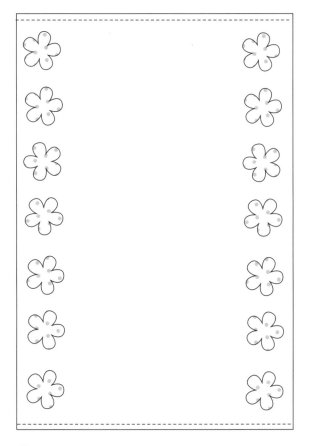

2 Press iron-on interfacing on to wrong side of polyester. Draw a flower shape on to the card and cut out. Use the shape to mark 14 flower outlines on the polyester. Cut out flowers. Stitch flowers to cloth along each long side at regular intervals as shown.

bobbly tray cloth

Inspired by flamboyant matador outfits, I have stitched cotton bobble trim around an old tea towel to make a great tray cloth. Now this would make a brilliant present for anyone from your granny to your brother who likes to entertain and wants to put a little 'ole' into their drinks parties. To capture the Spanish fiesta flavour, serve with glasses of ice cold fino sherry and bowls of hot, salted almonds.

MATERIALS
tea towel measuring
   67cm by 48cm
2.5m cotton bobble trim
sewing thread

1 With wrong side facing, pin or tack the cotton bobble trim all the way around the tea towel. Stitch as close to the edge as possible.

patchwork tablecloth

This crisp patchwork cloth with its chequer-board of pink gingham, plain white and floral cotton has a simple retro feeling. It provides just the right sort of decorative flourish when laying on a slap-up, old-fashioned tea with slices of toast and home-made cakes. If there are small children present, it might be wise to put a plastic sheet beneath the cloth so that the inevitable pools of spilt drink will not filter through and soak a delicate tabletop.

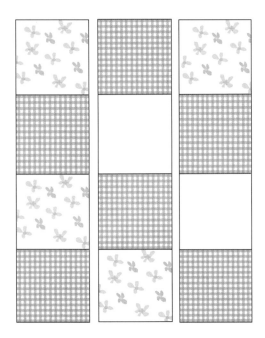

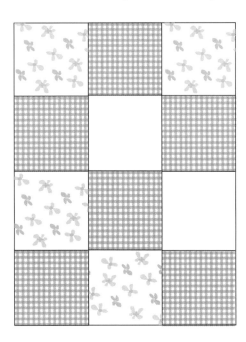

2 Stitch all three strips together lengthways with 1cm seams to make one piece. Press seams open.

1 Cut a total of 12 squares each measuring 43cm by 43cm from your scraps of gingham cotton, plain white cotton and floral cotton. Stitch the squares together randomly with 1cm seams into three strips of four squares. Press seams open. For a longer tablecloth, cut three more squares and add one more square to the end of each strip.

3 Turn and stitch 1cm hem all the way around. Press.

MATERIALS
the following makes a tablecloth measuring 123cm by 164cm

enough remnants from your workbag to make 12 (or 15) squares, each measuring 43cm by 43cm
sewing thread

waterproof picnic cloth

The great thing about picnicking is that you can do it anywhere, all year round – cold beers and barbeques on the beach in summer, hunky cheese sandwiches and soup from a thermos in winter. Without sounding wimpish, I think that the experience is altogether more pleasant if you can leave without a cold, damp posterior. Backing a smart blue and white check cloth with something waterproof – I chopped up some plasticised fabric found in a shop that supplies market traders – is, I guarantee you, the perfect solution.

MATERIALS
the following makes a cloth measuring 134cm by 134cm

140cm gingham cotton, 140cm wide
134cm by 134cm piece of waterproof
   plastic
sewing thread

1 Make sure the waterproof plastic is 3cm smaller all the way around than gingham cotton. Turn and stitch 1cm hem on all sides of gingham cotton. With wrong side of gingham cotton facing, pin or tack waterproof plastic in the centre.

2 To enclose the waterproof plastic, fold 2cm of the gingham cotton to the wrong side over the plastic all around the edge and pin or tack. Stitch close to the hem edge all the way around as shown.

flamenco tea cosy

Who cares if it's kitsch? Okay, I don't stretch to garden gnomes with fishing rods, but this spotty tea cosy will add 'allegria' to a teatime cuppa. The instructions are a little more involved than most in the book, but the design is basic: it's essentially a lined cover with frills and openings for the teapot's spout and handle. The wadding is inserted after the cosy has been stitched and turned right side out.

MATERIALS

the following makes one tea cosy

150cm polyester, at least 70cm wide

2 pieces wadding, cut 1cm less than A all the way around

2.8m bias binding, 12mm wide

sewing thread

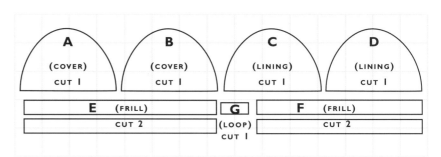

1 SQUARE = 10CM

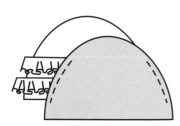

1 Trim all frills E and F with bias binding and gather frills (see Simple Sewing Techniques on pages 13 and 14). With right sides together, stitch one frill E to A with 1cm seam on lower edge as shown. Stitch on one frill F just above frill E.

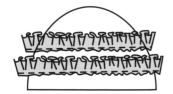

2 With right sides together, stitch lining C to A at the centre only of each side as shown. Turn right side out. Press. Repeat steps 1 and 2 with B, remaining frills and lining D.

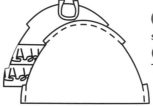

3 Make loop G using the same method as for ties (see Simple Sewing Techniques on page 13).

4 With right sides together, stitch A/C to B/D at bottom of sides and tops only, inserting loop as shown. Turn right side out. Press.

5 Insert layer of wadding in A/C and B/D. Fold 1cm to the inside around the open ends of A/C and B/D and pin or tack. Stitch close to edge to enclose wadding.

smart ideas for tables

ten best cut flowers

1 The heady scent of hyacinths is an intoxicating antidote to winter. I plant bulbs in the autumn for spring flowering or buy them ready cut from florists all year round.

2 I buy tiny, white, scented narcissi on slim green stems specially forced for Christmas time and plant them in flower pots with moss.

3 I like to cut roses from the garden, moist with dew. Pinkish white, delicately scented Mme Alfred Carriere and wild bright pink moss rose blooms are divine.

4 Sweetly scented old-fashioned stocks in pink and creamy whites are classic country garden flowers.

5 The best tulips are the white feathery parrot varieties, which look even more beautiful as they drop and open their frilly heads.

6 White tuberose buds on green stems have a sweet scent that intensifies as darkness falls. Five or six stems in a vase are all that's needed to finish off a simply laid table.

7 Big, blousy, pink peonies are my favourite and a sure sign that summer's here. In Spain I pick wild ones that grow in clumps amongst the chestnut groves.

8 Nasturtiums are easy to grow from seed, plus their brilliant orange and scarlet flowers look pretty in small glasses on the table. I also add the flowers to green salads for colour and their nutty peppery flavour.

9 The sunflower varieties with big saucer-sized heads sing out colour in the gloomiest of rooms. Use four or five in a large tank or vase to best effect.

10 Alliums with their leggy stems and fluffy balls in pink, white and various shades of blue and purple, look spare and architectural.

HOSTESS WITH THE MOSTESS

Thank goodness the yuppie days are over – when wannabe couples threw perfect dinner parties. How mad I must have been spending a day and a half reducing fish stock for fancy nouvelle cuisine mousselines that were gobbled up in a couple of minutes. These days entertaining is a far more relaxed affair, without fraught last-minute consultations with Delia. I aim to buy good ingredients and keep it simple: a bowl of steaming pasta with home-made tomato and basil sauce and freshly grated parmesan; or a good organically farmed chicken stuffed with herbs, lemon, onion and garlic, then roasted in the oven with lashings of potatoes.

TASTY TAPAS TREATS

Here are instant snackettes to accompany party drinks or when you need something delicious and nourishing, quickly. I always serve something sparkling at a party. If the budget doesn't run to Champagne, then Cordon Negro Spanish cava is equally delicious, and comes in sexy black bottles.

GOATS CHEESE ON TOAST Cut cheese into thin rounds and arrange on slices of ciabatta or baguette rubbed with olive oil and garlic and toasted on the other side. Grill until bubbling and brown.

QUAILS EGGS Buy in mini egg cartons from butchers or supermarkets, drop into boiling water and cook for 3 minutes. Rinse in cold water and serve on a plain white plate with a little bowl of salt, pepper and pimento as a tasty dip.

TOASTED SALTED ALMONDS Scatter blanched almonds on a baking tray and sprinkle with a little salt. Grill for a few minutes, turning once or twice. Serve immediately with with glasses of ice-cold dry Spanish Fino sherry.

SMOKED SALMON SANDWICHES Cut small squares of good brown bread, spread with a good lashing of cream cheese and layer with a thick slice of smoked salmon (organic if possible – not that dubious farmed stuff). Finish off with a squeeze of lemon and a good grinding of black pepper.

HUMOUS WITH CUMIN AND TOASTED PINENUTS Thick, garlicky humous eaten with hot pitta is almost a meal in itself. Process 400g drained chickpeas with a little of their water until smooth. Add 4 tablespoons tahini, 4 tablespoons olive oil, juice of 2 lemons, 6 chopped garlic cloves, 2 teaspoons ground cumin, 1 teaspoon of pimento or paprika and a handful of chopped coriander leaves. Sprinkle over a handful of toasted pinenuts to finish.

ASPARAGUS SPEARS Make sure you don't miss the asparagus season. Packed with minerals, it should be steamed rather than boiled to death so it remains crunchy and that rich green colour. Serve as many spears with melted butter as you can fit into your tummy.

SWEET AND STICKY

It's hard to go wrong serving up home-made cake or ice-cream for puddings and teatimes. I can't resist a slice of lemon sponge cake or some strawberry ice-cream made from my mother's recipe – it is completely idiot-proof and can be made without an ice-cream maker. Here are a couple of my favourite dead-easy recipes.

LEMON BUTTERCREAM CAKE

FOR THE CAKE	FOR THE ICING
250g butter, softened	150g butter
250g caster sugar	300g icing sugar
4 or 5 eggs, beaten	juice of 1 lemon
250g self-raising flour	grated rind of 1 lemon

Cream the butter and sugar together until light and fluffy. Add tablespoons of the beaten egg and flour alternately, finishing with the flour. Pour the sponge mixture into two well-greased 18cm cake tins. Bake in the middle of oven at 180°C for about 40 minutes. Test with a skewer – if it comes out clean the cake is done, if the mixture is still sticky it needs more cooking. Turn out sponges on to a wire rack and leave to cool.

To make the icing, melt the butter and pour into a food processor with the icing sugar and lemon juice and rind. Process until smooth. Sandwich the sponges together with a layer of icing and then use the remaining icing to cover the cake using a palette knife.

STRAWBERRY ICE CREAM

400g strawberries
200g caster sugar
284ml double cream

Chop the strawberries and process with the sugar in a mixer until smooth. Pour into a bowl. Whisk the double cream until thick and fold into the strawberry mixture. Freeze in a plastic box for a hour or so until ice forms around the edges. Remove and beat the part frozen mixture until creamy. Freeze or for another hour. Remove and beat again and return to the freezer. Serve wedged between wafers.

ten top kitchen items

❶ Stylish white china dinner plates and bowls are completely timeless. Look out for seconds at bargain prices in the sales. Catering shops that supply the restaurant and hotel trade are a source of robust and cheap white china.

❷ Simple streamlined stainless steel cutlery is fabulous to hold and looks good on a simply laid table.

❸ Unfussy ribbed glasses have a stylish utilitarian appeal that allows them to be used for quaffing at the most looks-conscious tables.

❹ Metal stove-top coffee pots – those wonderful little screwtop Italian gadgets – brew a kick-starting coffee in a few minutes.

❺ Wooden spoons in an assortment of sizes are a must – I keep mine stuffed in a flowerpot next to the gas hob.

❻ Food processor – I will not be parted from it for whizzing up everthing from gooey cakes to winter soups.

❼ Professional kitchen knives are essential for precision chopping. A small paring knife is particularly adaptable.

❽ Heavy-based ceramic pans make stove-top cooking easy. Mine are over twenty years old and inspire enormous contentment whenever I cook with them.

❾ Small wooden chopping boards are much easier to manoeuvre than a cumbersome butcher's block.

❿ Classic sixties Scandinavian mixing bowls come in gorgeous powder blue and are perfectly moulded with an integral pouring spout.

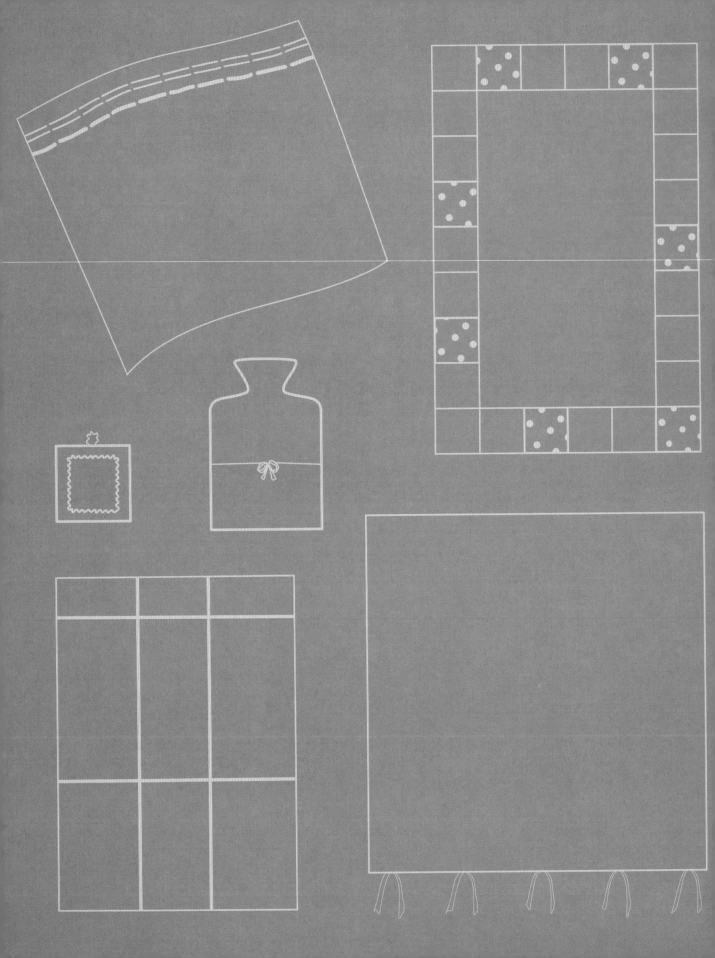

ten essential bedlinens

TUCK UP AT NIGHT WITH SHEETS TRIMMED WITH A POLKA-DOT EDGING, A PRETTY PATCHWORK

DUVET COVER OR A HOTTIE IN A SMART STRIPED TICKING COVER. RAID YOUR WORKBAG TO USE

BRIGHTLY COLOURED RIBBONS TO REVIVE WORN-OUT PILLOWCASES OR BLANKETS. AND SLIP

BETWEEN THE COVERS IN A SILK NIGHTIE OR COVER UP WITH A SIMPLE WRAP-AROUND ROBE.

SLEEP TIGHT!

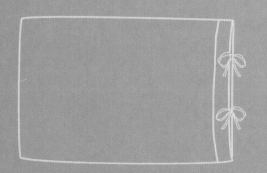

girlie pillowcases

If you can't afford a whole new set of bedlinen, yet fancy a new look for the boudoir, these pillowcases run up in candy pink linen and finished with gingham ribbon ties are a sweet and thrifty compromise. And what could be simpler than reviving a tired, but still serviceable, pillowcase that has been many times through the wash with rick-rack and ribbon, as I have done with the pretty blue and white one seen here. You will need approximately 260cm each of rick-rack and ribbon to edge a standard-size pillowcase.

MATERIALS

the following makes one pillowcase measuring 75cm by 50cm

120cm linen, at least 112cm wide
1.2m ribbon, 17mm wide
sewing thread

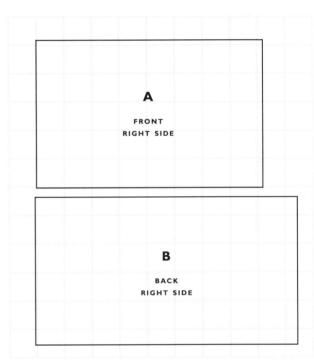

I SQUARE = 10CM

1 Turn and press 1cm then 5cm to the right side on one short side of A and pin or tack. Turn and press 1cm to wrong side of B and pin or tack. Stitch in place.

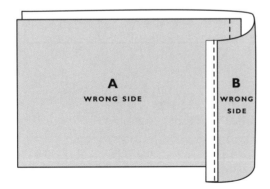

2 Place A and B with right sides together. Fold back excess length of B to wrong side over A. Pin or tack in place. Stitch 1cm seam on all three unhemmed sides, leaving hemmed end open (see Simple Sewing Techniques on page 15). Press.

3 Turn pillowcase right side out, ensuring flap of A is tucked inside. Press.

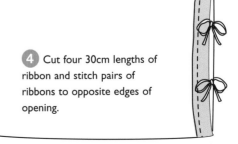

4 Cut four 30cm lengths of ribbon and stitch pairs of ribbons to opposite edges of opening.

irresistible silk nightie

I could not resist including a little indulgence in the form of this divine nightie – just the ticket for feeling gorgeous in the bedroom. Cut on the cross, this pattern will fit a UK size 12 and requires a little more skill than some of the other projects, as silk can be a quite challenging texture to work with. However, those who do not want to take the plunge could go foraging in a second-hand shop and revive a retro slip with fresh lace trim or new straps in thin slivers of silk ribbon.

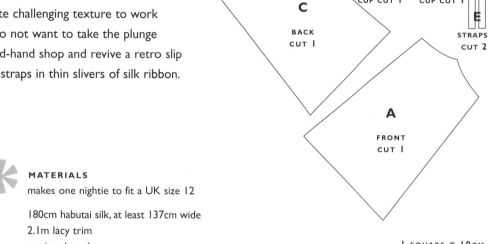

I SQUARE = 10CM

 MATERIALS

makes one nightie to fit a UK size 12

180cm habutai silk, at least 137cm wide
2.1m lacy trim
sewing thread

1 Overlock or zigzag stitch all raw edges.

2 Stitch darts in fronts B to make cups (see Simple Sewing Techniques on page 14). With right sides together, pin or tack front A to cups B as shown. Stitch 1cm seams.

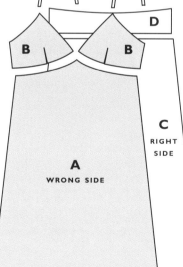

3 With right sides together, pin or tack backs C and D together. Stitch 1cm seam.

4 With right sides together, pin or tack front A/B to back C/D along sides. Stitch 1cm seams.

5 Make straps E using the same method as for ties (see Simple Sewing Techniques on page 13). Stitch straps in place as shown.

6 Turn slip dress right side out. Hang slip dress for two days to allow fabric to drop into place.

7 With right sides together, pin or tack lacy trim around top and bottom edges as shown. Stitch 1cm seams. Open out trim and topstitch on right side of silk close to trim seams.

spotty bordered topsheet

Professionally laundered monogrammed linen sheets might be the norm for royals and celebrities who snooze luxuriously in their posh beds, but what about us lesser mortals? If you want to make an individual style statement on a shoestring, yet feel just as pampered and stylish tucked up in a suburban semi with the Sunday newspapers and egg soldiers, how about trimming sheets with your own signature print, pattern or colour. This flamenco spot pattern is my current passion.

MATERIALS
cotton sheet for a single or
    double bed
60cm cotton, at least 112cm wide
    for single-bed sheet or at least
    137cm wide for double-bed
    sheet
sewing thread

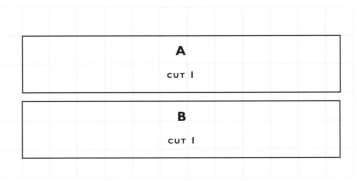

I SQUARE = 10CM

1 With right sides together, stitch A and B together at ends with 1cm seam so strip is wide enough to cover width of sheet to be bordered. Press seam open.

2 Turn and press 1cm to wrong side along two long edges of joined strip A/B.

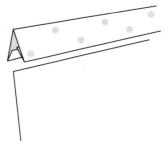

3 Fold strip A/B in half widthways with wrong sides together and press. Insert sheet inside the folded strip A/B. Pin or tack in place.

4 Trim and fold open ends to the inside at sides of border. Pin or tack in place. Stitch all along border, close to edge, to secure.

patched duvet cover

According to the principles of wise camping, a thermal sleeping bag is the most practical type of bedding. On a hot midsummer's night, however, when the mood is more romantic and conditions kind, cuddle up under this patched cover slipped over a cosy duvet. Just think, you could be the envy of your next-door-tent neighbours at this year's music festival – provided it doesn't pour down.

MATERIALS

the following makes a duvet cover 148cm wide by 198cm long

420cm cotton calico, 150cm wide
enough remnants from your workbag to make
  26 squares, each measuring 22cm by 22cm
sewing thread
1.5m touch-and-close tape

1 With right sides together, stitch patchwork squares together with 1cm seams to form a rectangular border as shown. Press seams open. Turn and stitch 1cm hems around inner and outer edge of patchwork border.

A/B

FRONT AND BACK
CUT 2

C   SQUARES
      CUT 26

1 SQUARE = 10CM

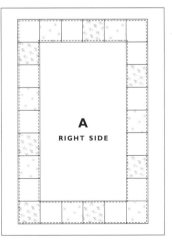

A

RIGHT SIDE

2 Pin or tack stitched patchwork to centre of right side of A. Topstitch the border in place close to the inner and outer edges.

3 With right sides together, pin or tack A to B. Stitch 1cm seam along three sides. Turn and stitch 1cm hem around the opening. Turn cover right side out. Press.

A

WRONG SIDE

4 Attach strips of touch-and-close tape to both sides of the open end to fasten.

bo-ho blanket

Good-quality chocolate, hot water on tap and a humble woollen blanket are just a few of life's essential creature comforts. I have a stash of favourite blankets that have been passed down over the years by mothers or have been picked up in sales. I give tired, worn blankets a new lease of life with a kind of laid-back, bo-ho look. After gentle laundering with a wool-friendly detergent, I conceal any ragged edges with satin binding and add strips of bright velvet – pink and lime green is a yummy combination – in rows or criss-cross patterns.

MATERIALS

woollen blanket measuring
   160cm by 120cm
6.2m satin, at least 8cm wide,
   for binding
2.5m velvet ribbon, 2.5–3cm wide
4m velvet ribbon in contrasting
   colour, 2.5–3cm wide
sewing thread

1 Pin or tack velvet ribbons to right side of blanket, running the length and width of the blanket as shown. Topstitch ribbons close to the edges to secure.

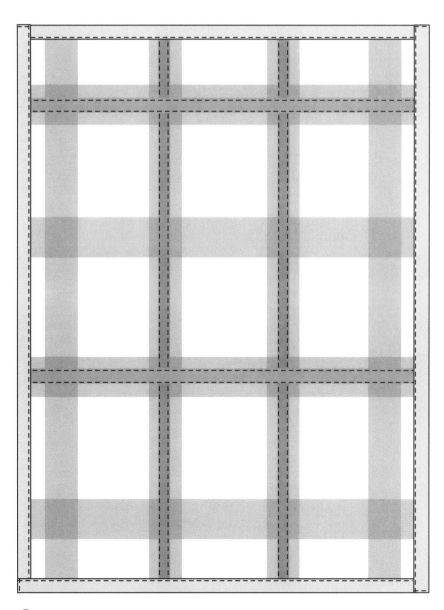

2 Bind outer edge of blanket with satin ribbon (see Simple Sewing Techniques on page 15).

pretty cotton blanket

Noted for its lightweight and warm qualities, the woven cotton cellular blanket is a worthy staple of matron's linen cupboard and is employed in every hospital for bundling tender newborns. All very admirable but hardly stylish. So hey, what's this gorgeous ribboned lavender throw? Yes, you've guessed! And it is simply achieved with a useful little packet of fabric dye suitable for using in the washing machine and some pretty ribbon. Woven cotton blankets are modestly priced and available in most department stores.

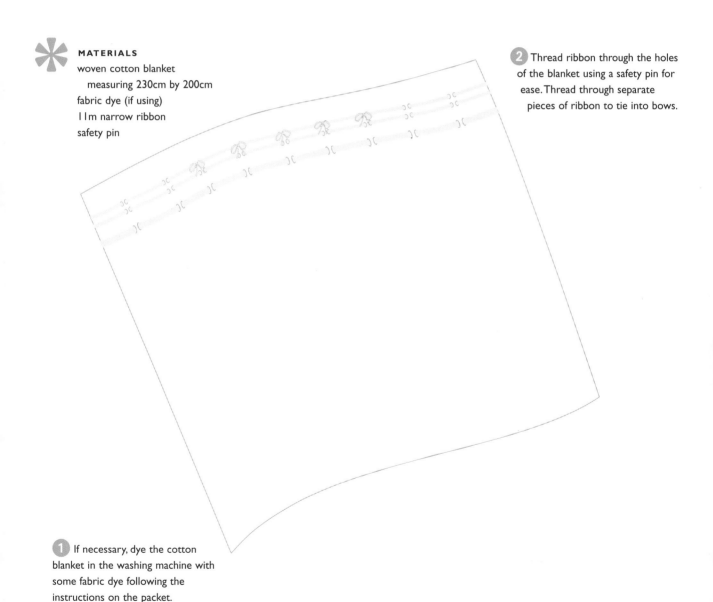

MATERIALS

woven cotton blanket
    measuring 230cm by 200cm
fabric dye (if using)
11m narrow ribbon
safety pin

2 Thread ribbon through the holes of the blanket using a safety pin for ease. Thread through separate pieces of ribbon to tie into bows.

1 If necessary, dye the cotton blanket in the washing machine with some fabric dye following the instructions on the packet.

luscious lavender bag

In summer I pick sprigs of herby, aromatic lavender from my garden to spread on sheets of newspaper and dry in the sun. It's then a matter of running up lavender bags in whatever remnant of fabric I have to hand – this one was cut from a worn-out fifties apron I found at a jumble sale. I squash the finished lavender bags in drawers for fragrant knickers or hang them amongst my best clothes to repel a moth assault.

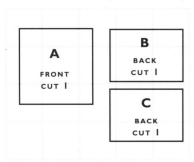

I SQUARE = 10CM

MATERIALS
the following makes one bag measuring 18cm by 18cm

40cm cotton, at least 60cm wide
80cm rick-rack trim
sewing thread

1 Pin or tack rick-rack trim to right side of A, 3–4cm from the edges as shown. Stitch along centre of rick-rack to secure.

2 Turn and stitch 1cm hem on one long side of both B and C.

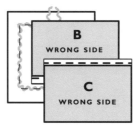

3 With right sides together, layer B and C on A as shown and pin. Sandwich a hanging loop between the layers and pin or tack.

4 Stitch 1cm seam around all four sides. Turn bag right side out. Press.

5 To secure the lavender, make an inner bag from calico by cutting two pieces 18cm by 18cm, stitching on three sides, turning right side out, filling with lavender and then turning under open edges and stitching to secure. Place lavender-filled inner bag inside rick-rack trimmed outer bag.

all-purpose wrap

When an element of early morning decency is required, it is always useful to have a simple wrap to hand. The lighter the wrap the better: teddy-bear thick towelling robes are great but restrict movement and are best for lolling around in the health club. Cotton, linen or silk take up the minimum amount of space in a suitcase when travelling.

1 Make belt, belt carriers and hanging loop using the same method as for ties (see Simple Sewing Techniques on page 13), but leave ends open.

2 With right sides together, stitch back A and fronts B and C together at shoulders with 1cm seams. Stitch sleeves D and E to main body A/B/C.

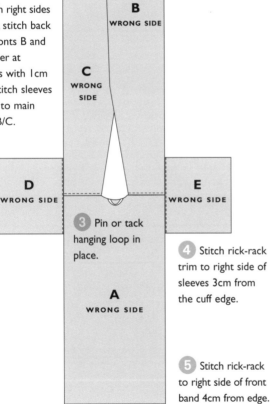

3 Pin or tack hanging loop in place.

4 Stitch rick-rack trim to right side of sleeves 3cm from the cuff edge.

5 Stitch rick-rack to right side of front band 4cm from edge.

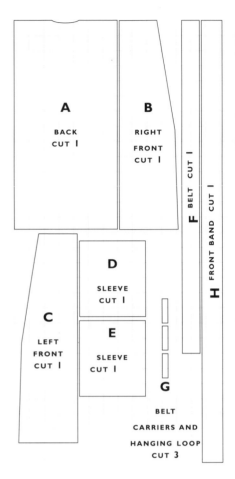

1 SQUARE = 10CM

6 Stitch band to front edges and neck of wrap as shown, using the binding technique (see Simple Sewing Techniques on page 14). Trim off excess at ends.

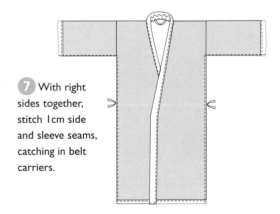

7 With right sides together, stitch 1cm side and sleeve seams, catching in belt carriers.

8 Turn and stitch 1cm hems on sleeves and bottom edge of wrap. Turn wrap right side out. Press.

MATERIALS

the following makes one medium-size wrap

320cm lightweight cotton, 150cm wide
4m rick-rack trim
sewing thread

gingham duvet cover

It is frustrating that fabrics wide enough to make double duvet covers or sheeting are generally only available in retail shops in a limited selection of plain colours. As a lover of woven gingham cottons that are only available in narrow widths, I suggest the invisible seam technique as a solution for making bedlinens. This gingham duvet cover is made from a sheet and two lengths of 112cm-wide gingham sewn together with an invisible seam. If you want to attempt a single version, then, of course, you need one panel of 137cm-wide gingham cotton.

MATERIALS

the following makes one duvet cover measuring 200cm by 202cm

450m gingham cotton, 112cm wide
cotton sheet for a double bed
sewing thread

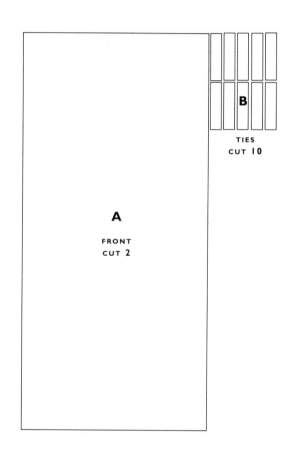

A

FRONT
CUT 2

B

TIES
CUT 10

I SQUARE = 10CM

1 With right sides together, pin or tack two fronts A together along one long side. Stitch 1cm seam. Press seam open.

2 Trim sheet to same size as A. With right sides together, pin or tack A to sheet. Stitch 1cm seam on three sides.

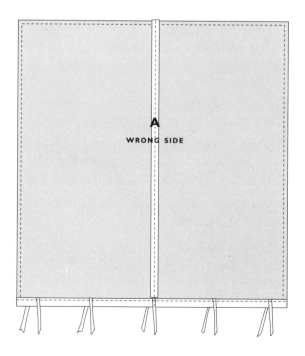

A

WRONG SIDE

3 Make ten ties (see Simple Sewing Techniques on page 13). For hem along opening, turn and press 3.5cm to wrong side twice. Pin or tack in place. Then pin or tack pairs of ties along opposite edges of opening. Stitch hem and ties in place. Turn cover right side out. Press.

ticking hottie cover

On breath-stopping icy winter nights it is a delicious feeling to slide beneath sheets warmed by a hot-water bottle. Low-tech and functional, this household item features in just about every interior accessories collection with covers in everything from linen to fake fur. Here is a basic pattern for a hottie cover to make yourself, much cheaper than a shop-bought one and a brilliant idea for DIY Christmas or birthday presents. Personalise your gift by using the recipient's favourite fabric.

MATERIALS

the following makes one hot-water bottle cover measuring 43cm by 30cm:

130cm cotton ticking, at least 50cm wide
30cm ribbon, 1cm wide
sewing thread

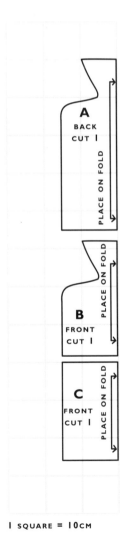

2 With right sides together, layer B and C on A and pin or tack. Stitch 1cm seam all the way around.

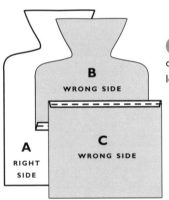

1 Turn and stitch 1cm hem on straight side of B and one long side of C. Press.

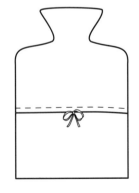

3 Turn cover right side out. Press. Cut two 15cm lengths of ribbon and stitch one to each side of the opening to make a tie.

1 SQUARE = 10CM

smart ideas for beds

ten tips for bedding

FILLINGS FOR PILLOWS AND DUVETS:

1 Duck feathers make firm to medium firm pillows.

2 Duck down is lighter and softer than the feather fills, yet supportive and comfortable.

3 Goose down is even lighter and softer than duck down, and the most luxurious, and hence costliest filling.

4 There are also anti-allergenic fillings for allergy sufferers.

PROPER CARE WILL KEEP YOUR BED IN GOOD CONDITION. AIM FOR THE FOLLOWING:

5 Protect mattress and pillows with a cotton mattress cover (prevents embarrasing stains that you don't want the cleaner to see).

6 On waking, throw back the bed clothes and leave the bed to air for 20 minutes to allow body moisture to evaporate.

7 Turn the mattress over from side to side and end to end every few months (enlist help from muscly body) to make mattress filling distribute evenly and prevent sagging potholes where you lie.

8 Obvious, but diffcult to police – don't let children bounce on beds.

9 When moving, never roll up or squash a mattress to transport it as you'll wreck it.

10 Vacuum the mattress from time to time to remove fluff and dust.

AND SO TO BED...

Among my earlier jobs as a photographic stylist were a number of shoots to advertise the latest ranges for various bedding manufacturers. I came to dread them as we had to dress the beds with mounds of unnecessary pillows, valances that looked like hovercraft skirts and sheets that had to be ironed and smoothed to perfection. Why post-production couldn't airbrush out tiny creases afterwards I never knew, instead of putting me through torture by steam machine. Having made a really nasty polyester pillowcase look perkier than it deserved with my cleverly disguised piece of sticky tape, the photographer would pipe up, 'Yeah looks cool, but that bit on the right could do with a little more tweaking.' Knowing I was at extreme risk of vaporising my styling fee, I'd keep the unrepeatable expletives to myself. The client would look on oblivious to the on-set angst.

In my opinion, a bed should be voluptuous and sensuous, like a freshly picked peach. Tangled linen sheets and carelessly folded soft woollen blankets are far more tempting than the stiff exhibits in some catalogues. My advice for a well-dressed bed is to choose natural textures: crisp white cotton sheets; linen sheets, if you can afford them (second-hand examples, sometimes never used and bought up by dealers from house sales are good value and are often much and hardier than linen woven today); and blankets – wool for winter and cotton for summer – to layer. Forget great banks of pillows and cushions. You would be better spending your money on a few good goosedown pillows for really comfortable sleep.

HANDY HINTS FOR BUYING A BED

When buying a bed it is important to consider several points to make sure you get the right bed for you. Bear in mind the following:

TRY it for size, together if it's a bed for two.

THINK big as larger beds are more comfortable, especially if you are joined in the night by extra companions (the under-fives).

GET the correct support and comfort for your weight and build.

BUY an interior-sprung mattress for comfort, the more springs the better the support.

GO low for a modern look. A basic patform with a mattress is the preferred look for urban dwellers.

CHOOSE wooden or metal bedframes on legs with airy space beneath for a country feel.

PAINT the bedframe in the same colour as the bedroom walls for a unified look.

STORE a fold up Z-bed in a cupboard for unexpected guests if space is limited.

HANDY HINTS FOR LOOKING AFTER BEDLINENS

MEND any tears or split seams before washing sheets and pillowcases.

REMOVE any stains before laundering in fresh hot soapy water.

DON'T hang out sheets to dry in a fierce wind or they may be whipped into holes, especially if they've worn thin.

IRON linens whilst damp; in fact, the heavier the linen the damper it should be for ironing.

FOLD sheets and pillowcases flat as they are taken off the line. When ready to iron, if necessary, sprinkle them lightly and evenly with water. (I have some aromatic orange flower water from Angela Flanders, and have decanted it into a plastic spray bottle to scent my sheets.)

FOLD sheets evenly and then press the creases in by hand. Folds should not be ironed into bedlinen.

IRON pillowcases from the edge inwards.

AIR bedlinen before storing in a warm, dry cupboard. If sheets or pillowcases become yellowed, rewash and dry in sunlight, which has wonderful whitening qualities.

WASH blankets on a wool cycle with a gentle detergent in the washing-machine. If there is no machine, wash blankets in the bath with a mild detergent and tread them with bare feet. Avoid over-rubbing or they become hard and felted. Rinse in three changes of water and squeeze out any excess. Dry over parallel lines on a collapsible airer. Ironing is not necessary. Air before using or storing.

STORE linen amongst sachets of dried lavender to impart a gorgeous scent.

DETER moths from eating your best blankets by putting a mixture of lavender, cloves, cinnamon, black pepper and orris root in a muslin bag. Cedar-wood balls also have a similar moth-deterrent effect.

ten tips for sleeping well

❶ Programme your body and go to bed and get up at roughly the same time each day (except those with small children).

❷ Your bedroom should be neither too hot nor too cold, and as quiet and dark as possible. The ideal temperature for sleep is 16°C.

❸ Take exercise. Even a 20-minute brisk walk each day is a great stress reliever, although not recommended just before bed or you'll be overstimulated.

❹ Don't order a double espresso after dinner or you'll be buzzing into the early hours. I never drink coffee after 4pm.

❺ Wear earplugs to drown out noisy neighbours or a snoring bed mate.

❻ Lay off the hard stuff; alcohol sends you into instant stupor but will interrupt sleep later on in the night.

❼ It goes without saying that relaxing before bed will help you sleep, even if all you can manage is a bath and the newspaper headlines.

❽ If sleep eludes you, counting sheep is actually less productive than getting up and doing some light task.

❾ A hot-water bottle keeps the chill factor off in winter and helps you to drop off.

❿ A friend gave me a little bag of South American worry dolls that I keep under my pillow. I swear they have induced some better nights sleep.

ten essential accessories

Add to your wardrobe with a trimmed cardie, a little halter-neck top or a pretty gingham a-line skirt. Bags are always useful, so try the sew easy ideas for a useful laundry bag, a great big beach bag and a pretty polka dot shopper. Be resourceful and rescue a pair of old jeans with hippy-style floral fabric patches.

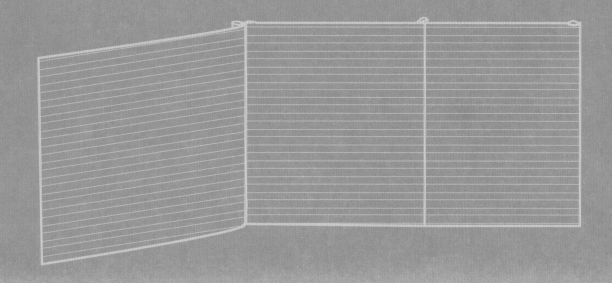

patchwork bag

So much more glamorous than a plastic carrier, this hard-wearing patchwork bag in a variety of spots, checks and plains can be used to transport everything from work files to supper ingredients. It consists of an outer bag constructed from patch pieces of fabric and a lining – just like the big green beach bag on pages 142 and 143 – for extra strength and to improve the general appearance of the bag itself.

MATERIALS

the following makes one bag measuring 39cm wide by 32cm deep

enough remnants from your workbag to make 12 patchwork squares measuring 15cm by 15cm and 6 patchwork rectangles measuring 15cm by 8cm
50cm by 40cm piece of canvas, for handles
60cm cotton, at least 90cm wide, for lining
1.7m rick-rack trim
sewing thread

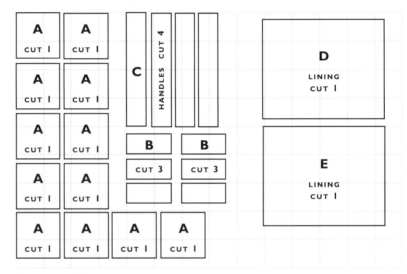

1 SQUARE = 10CM

1 With right sides together, stitch three patchwork squares together with 1cm seams. Repeat with three more patchwork squares, and then three patchwork rectangles. Press seams open. Stitch three strips together with 1cm seams as shown. Press seams open. Stitch rick-rack to right side of patchwork along top seam as shown.

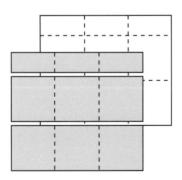

2 Repeat step 1 with remaining patchwork pieces. With right sides of patchworks together, stitch 1cm seam along three sides. Turn bag right side out. Press.

3 To make the lining, with right sides of D and E together, stitch 1cm seam on three sides. Turn 1cm hem. Press.

4 Make handles C as for making ties (see Simple Sewing Techniques on page 13). Stitch rick-rack on to the centre of one side of handles. Sandwich handles between lining and bag. Pin or tack handles in place on opposite sides of the lining.

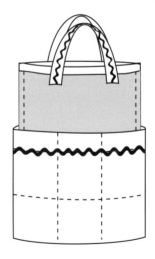

5 Turn 1cm to wrong side at top of patchwork and pin or tack. Pin or tack top edge of lining to edge of bag. Stitch as close to the top edge as possible. If desired, stitch handles to bag with re-inforced stitching (see Simple Sewing Techniques on page 15).

stripey windbreak

Although it is often associated with all that's uncool about British beach culture – peeling pink flesh, fish-paste sandwiches and knotted hankies – the windbreak, fashioned in a nice brightly striped canvas, is a mainstay of essential seaside equipment. I cannot recommend the practical virtues of a windbreak too highly: use it to fend off the wind, create a little camp-cum-suntrap, and to eat your smoked salmon and cream cheese bagels without a tonne of sand blowing into them. Remember to take a mallet to ensure that your windbreak is pitched properly.

MATERIALS
the following makes one windbreak
 approximately 108cm by 172cm

200cm by 110cm piece of canvas
4 broom handles, 2.5cm in
 diameter
strong sewing thread

1 Turn and stitch 1cm hems on all raw edges.

4 To enclose broom handles at top, stitch across four top openings.

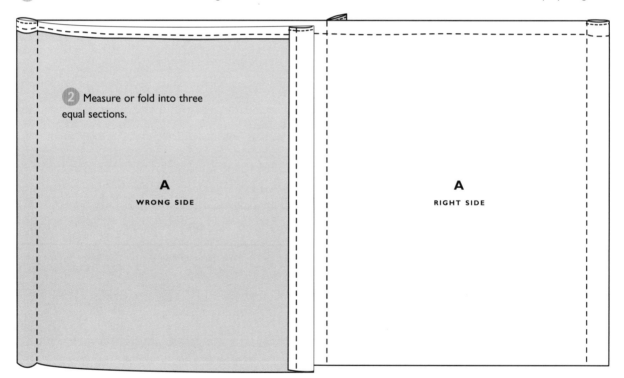

2 Measure or fold into three equal sections.

A

WRONG SIDE

A

RIGHT SIDE

3 With right sides together, stitch 4cm in from the crease of both folds to make pockets for the broom handles. Similarly, turn 5cm hem in from each end and stitch 4cm in from fold.

big canvas beach bag

When devising this roomy bag I was inspired by the oversized carriers that Ikea supply to shoppers for loading their buys. Large enough to accommodate assorted paraphenalia – buckets, spades, towels, edible goodies – for the beach or picnicking in the park, a bag with short handles like this one can be carried with comfort between two people or easily slung over the shoulder (bags with long handles have the habit of banging against hips when walking). You could make an unlined version, but I think that a lined bag not only is more substantial, it looks more finished and stylish.

MATERIALS

the following makes one bag measuring 35cm wide by 55cm long by 35cm deep

200cm cotton canvas, at least 90cm wide, for bag

200cm polyester, at least 90cm wide, for lining

sewing thread

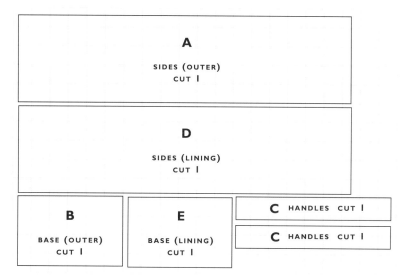

A
SIDES (OUTER)
CUT 1

D
SIDES (LINING)
CUT 1

B
BASE (OUTER)
CUT 1

E
BASE (LINING)
CUT 1

C HANDLES CUT 1

C HANDLES CUT 1

1 SQUARE = 10CM

1 With right sides together, stitch ends of A together with 1cm seam to form a ring. With right sides of A and B together, stitch 1cm seam. Turn right side out. Press.

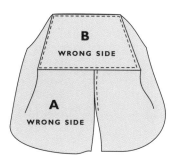

B
WRONG SIDE

A
WRONG SIDE

2 Make handles C using same method as for making ties (see Simple Sewing Techniques on page 13).

3 Turn and press 10cm hem to wrong side on bag to accommodate handles. Pin or tack handles in place on opposite sides of the bag. Stitch handles to bag with square and diagonal re-inforced stitching (see Simple Sewing Techniques on page 15).

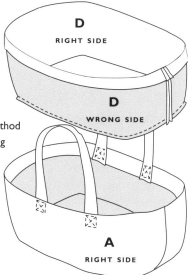

D
RIGHT SIDE

D
WRONG SIDE

A
RIGHT SIDE

4 To make the lining, repeat step 1, but using D and E and leaving lining inside out. Turn and press 10cm hem to wrong side. Pin or tack top edge of lining to inside top edge of bag. Stitch all the way around as close to the top edge as possible.

cotton laundry bag

There will be no excuse for leaving a week's supply of dirty socks under the bed if you have a go at making this decent-sized laundry bag. If there are a number of people in your family, you could make several bags and embroider initials on each or sew on name tapes normally used for identifying childrens' school uniforms. You could scale this laundry bag down for children, which could be useful for encouraging good domestic habits. This laundry bag has handles, which makes it less of a hassle to fill than the drawstring variety that has to be pulled open.

1 Turn and press 1cm then 2cm to wrong side on short side of A and B and pin or tack. Stitch in place.

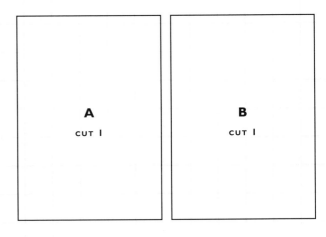

A

CUT 1

B

CUT 1

1 SQUARE = 10CM

2 With right sides together, pin or tack A to B. Stitch 1cm seam around three unhemmed sides, leaving the top open. Turn bag right side out. Press.

3 Pin or tack cotton webbing to right side of bag, 1cm from top edge. Secure webbing with a line of stitching as close as possible to each edge.

4 To make straps, cut two 80cm lengths of webbing. Fold under ends of webbing and sew to bag with a square and diagonal shape for extra strength (see Simple Sewing Techniques on page 15).

MATERIALS

the following makes one bag measuring 50cm wide by 68cm tall

90cm medium-weight cotton, at least 112cm wide
3m white cotton webbing, 2.5cm wide, for handles
sewing thread

roll-up garden toolkit

This part-bag, part-folder is a really practical way of consolidating basic garden tools such as fork, trowel, dibber, seed labels and garden twine. The idea came to mind when my chef brother-in-law came to stay with his wonderful repertoire of cakes and formidable batterie of knives, rolled up in a tough white canvas model as used by those in the catering trade. Using the same principle I have made versions adjusting the size of pockets for paintbrushes and basic sewing tools.

MATERIALS

the following makes one toolkit case measuring 30cm by 60cm

60cm gingham cotton, at least 90cm wide
2.8m bias binding, 2cm wide
1m ribbon, 2cm wide
sewing thread

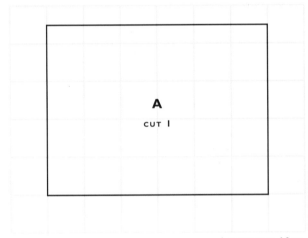

A

CUT 1

1 SQUARE = 10CM

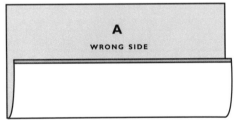

A

WRONG SIDE

1 Bind lower edge of A with bias binding (see Simple Sewing Techinques on page 15).

2 Fold one third of A to wrong side lengthways to make flap. Press flat and pin or tack flap in place at edges.

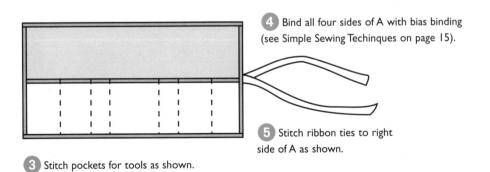

4 Bind all four sides of A with bias binding (see Simple Sewing Techinques on page 15).

5 Stitch ribbon ties to right side of A as shown.

3 Stitch pockets for tools as shown.

adaptable a-line skirt

This is a most versatile skirt for your wardrobe. As long as the fabric is good quality and the colour or print striking, the simplicity of the pattern allows you wear a few trendy accessories. Lightweight cotton, silk or linen are all textures to consider, and the blue gingham here suits the current fifties retro look. This basic A-line shape can be dressed up with heels or down with laid-back flat sandals. This light gathered skirt (the trick is to use fine and narrow elastic to prevent ugly bunching) fits a UK size 12.

MATERIALS

the following makes one skirt to fit a UK size 12

140cm gingham cotton, 112cm wide
1m elastic, 1cm wide
sewing thread
safety pin

2 To make the waistband casing, turn over and press 2cm to wrong side twice around top edge and pin or tack. Stitch, leaving a small opening at the centre of front A for threading through the elastic.

1 With right sides together, pin or tack A to B along sides. Stitch 1cm seams.

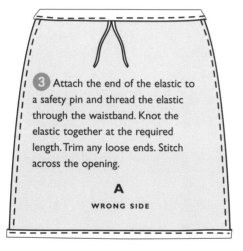

3 Attach the end of the elastic to a safety pin and thread the elastic through the waistband. Knot the elastic together at the required length. Trim any loose ends. Stitch across the opening.

A

WRONG SIDE

4 Try on the skirt and pin to the required length. Turn and stitch hem at bottom edge of skirt where pinned.

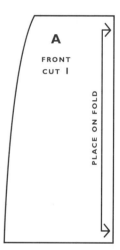

A

**FRONT
CUT 1**

PLACE ON FOLD

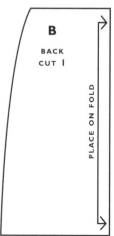

B

**BACK
CUT 1**

PLACE ON FOLD

1 SQUARE = 10CM

hand-dyed cardigan with trim

This sassy vintage-style cardigan is the result of trawling through the bargain bin at an extraordinary discount shop across the road from my flat. 'Quality at affordable prices' is the boast plastered across the windows, and, indeed, I've seen Prada leather seconds at knock-down prices. My quest: to find a basic white thermal cardigan at a fraction of it's normal price. Having struck lucky, I cut off the nasty lace trim and dyed the cardigan in the washing-machine using the same mint green I used for the All-purpose Wrap on pages 128 and 129. I then sewed on some pretty broderie anglaise trim and, finally, attached ribbon ties.

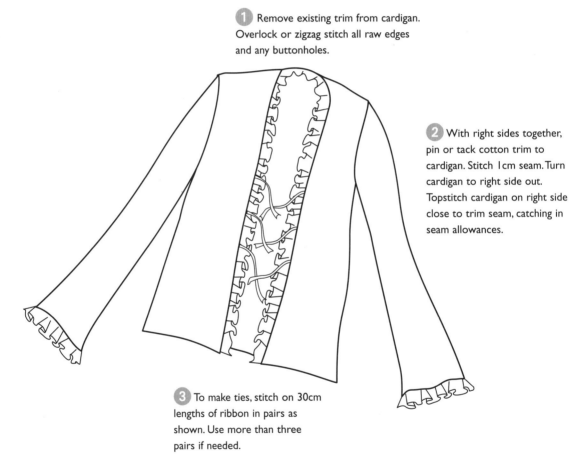

1 Remove existing trim from cardigan. Overlock or zigzag stitch all raw edges and any buttonholes.

2 With right sides together, pin or tack cotton trim to cardigan. Stitch 1cm seam. Turn cardigan to right side out. Topstitch cardigan on right side close to trim seam, catching in seam allowances.

3 To make ties, stitch on 30cm lengths of ribbon in pairs as shown. Use more than three pairs if needed.

MATERIALS

thermal cotton cardigan
200cm broderie anglaise cotton trim
3m ribbon, 6–10mm wide
sewing thread

patched hippie jeans

Customising a pair of old denims – seventies style with flowery patches on a worn-out knee or back pocket – is a groovy but also an eminently practical solution for giving extra life to worn-out but still serviceable items. As peasant-smocked and patchouli-scented models float dreamily across the fashion pages of magazines, the current hippy revival in fashion seems to reflect the current eco-conscious, pro-peace mood. I am also pleased to note that as school fees shoot into the stratosphere there's no shame amongst today's financially stretched parents who send their offspring to school with hand-me-down and many times repaired uniforms.

MATERIALS
your favourite pair of
    denims
remants from your workbag
rick-rack trim
sewing thread

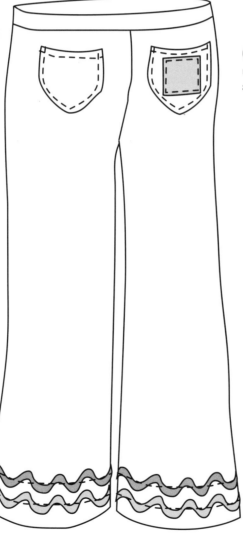

1 Stitch seventies-style patches and rick-rack trim to denims to give them a new lease of life.

sexy halter top

It is always the adorable little top with a must-have label that's the most expensive thing in the shop. So if you're fed up with window-shopping and want a fresh look for summer, why not have a go and make this simple little halter-neck tie top – an accessory that is fashionproof and will always work with whatever the latest pants shape or length of hem. With an absence of supporting features, this pattern is not recommended for ample bosoms.

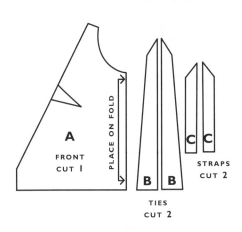

MATERIALS
the following makes one halter top
to fit a UK size 12

90cm tana lawn cotton, 112cm wide
5m bias binding, 2cm wide
sewing thread

I SQUARE = 10CM

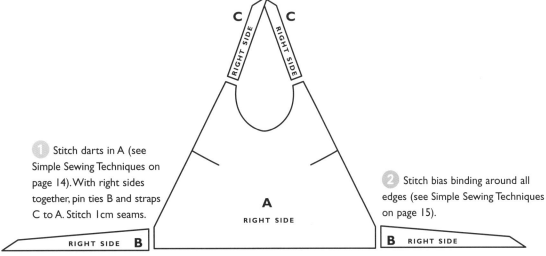

1 Stitch darts in A (see Simple Sewing Techniques on page 14). With right sides together, pin ties B and straps C to A. Stitch 1cm seams.

2 Stitch bias binding around all edges (see Simple Sewing Techniques on page 15).

floppy patchwork hat

Using the patchwork theme for a hat is a good way to use up fabric scraps and to produce a really individual present for a godchild or one of your own. I have found in my experience that no one can ever have too many hats. As a scatter-brained mother-of-three, I know that they are one of the common items of clothing to be left behind on the bus, or blown overboard on a family outing, or eaten by a pony, the fate that befell my favourite Spanish sun hat. Note that this particular design has the virtue of sitting firmly over the head and doesn't necessitate ties. This hat will fit an average-size female head.

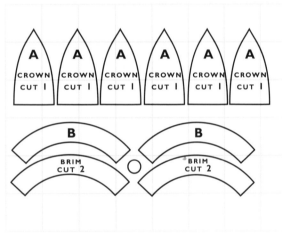

I SQUARE = 10CM

MATERIALS

the following makes one medium-size hat

remnants of cotton fabric, each at least
    11cm by 22cm
kit for making 1 fabric-covered button
    3cm in diameter
sewing thread

1 With right sides together, pin or tack pieces A together along side seams as shown. Stitch 1cm seams. Press seams open. Turn hat right side out.

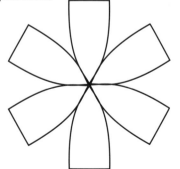

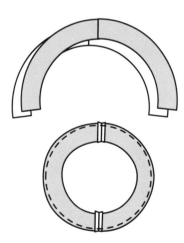

2 With right sides together, stitch brim B pieces together with 1cm seams to make two circles. Press seams open.

3 With right sides together, pin or tack two brim B circles together around outer edges. Stitch 1cm seam.

4 With right sides together, pin or tack brim to hat. Stitch 1cm seam.

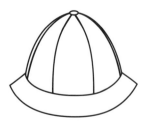

5 Turn brim down. Cover button and stitch to top of hat.

stockists and suppliers

FABRICS, TRIMMINGS AND OTHER SEWING ACCESSORIES

Barnett Lawson Trimmings Ltd
16–17 Little Portland Street
London W1W 8NE
Tel: 020 7636 8591
www.bltrimmings.com
A huge selection of ribbons and braids

The Blue Door
74 Church Road
London SW13 0DQ
Tel: 020 8748 9785
Plains, stripes and checks in cotton and linen

J.W. Bollom & Co. Ltd
Head Office
Croydon Road
Beckenham
Kent BR3 4BL
Tel: 020 8658 2299 for stockists
Large colour range of flameproof felts (bright pink, green, blue, white are just a few) and muslins

The Button Queen
19 Marylebone Lane
London W1M 5FE
Tel: 020 7935 1505
www.thebuttonqueen.co.uk
It's impossible to describe the range of buttons stocked here, suffice to say that it is diverse enough to suit most requirements

The Cloth Shop
290 Portobello Road
London W10 5TE
Tel: 020 8968 6001
www.clothshop.co.uk
Everything from winter wools to summer stripes; plenty of natural fibres such as jute, wool and silk, all well priced. It also stocks sari silks and antique linen

The Conran Shop
Michelin House
81 Fulham Road
London SW3 6RD
Tel: 020 7589 7401
www.conran.com
Plains, stripes and checks in cotton and linen, and a good colour range in cotton velvet

Designer's Guild
267–271 & 275–277 King's Road
London SW3 5EN
Tel: 020 7351 5775
Tel: 020 7243 7300 for enquiries
www.designersguild.com
Fresh stripes, checks and florals. Light sheer organzas, cottons and linen, as well as felt and wool

G.P. & J. Baker
Chelsea Harbour Design Centre
London SW10 0XF
Tel: 020 7351 7760
www.gpjbaker.co.uk
Modern upholstery fabrics, as well as traditional. Plain fabrics in different weaves and textures, from wool and cashmere to light cotton voiles

Ian Mankin
109 Regents Park Road
London NW1 8UR
Tel: 020 7722 0997
Tel: 020 7722 0997 for mail order
Excellent utility fabrics; tickings, stripes and checks, from fine cotton ginghams to heavy linen in butchers stripes, plain coloured cottons and linens. All fabrics reasonably priced

Ikea
Brent Park
2 Drury Way
North Circular Road
London NW10 0TH
Tel: 020 8208 5600 for enquiries
www.ikea.co.uk
Bargain fabrics in simple stripes, checks and plain colours, plus ready-made curtains, cushions and blinds

International Textile Co. Ltd
Firth Mill
Skipton
North Yorkshire BD23 2RL
Tel: 01756 793941
Good selection of cottons, linens and velvets and in a range of plain colours

John Lewis
278–306 Oxford Street
London W1 1EX
Tel: 020 7629 7711 for enquiries
www.johnlewis.com
Great fabric departments selling silk, muslin, canvas, ticking and other utility

textiles. Ribbons, buttons, felt squares, beads, cotton, zips and other sewing accessories, including fabric dyes, polystyrene fillings for beanbags and sewing machines. Good selection of roller and roman blinds

K.A. International
68 Sloane Avenue
London SW3 3DD
Tel: 020 7584 7352
www.ka-international.com
Huge range of good value fabrics including stripes, checks and prints, woven and textured fabrics

Laura Ashley
27 Bagleys Lane
London SW6 2QA
Tel: 0870 5622 116 for stockists
Tel: 0800 868 100 for mail order
www.lauraashley.com
Stripes, checks and florals in a good choice of colours

Liberty plc
Regent Street
London W1R 6AH
Tel: 020 7734 1234
www.liberty.co.uk
Look amongst the dress fabrics for classic, lightweight, floral tana lawns for floaty curtains, pillows and bags

MacCulloch & Wallis
25–26 Dering Street
London W1S 1AT
Tel: 020 7491 2481
www.macculloch-wallis.com
Mecca for home sewers. Downstairs there are bolts and bolts of gorgeous stuffs, with knowledgeable staff who are generous with cuttings. Go upstairs for trimmings – fabulous ribbons and bindings, plus general sewing tools and accessories

Malabar
31–33 South Bank Business Centre
Ponton Road
London SW8 5BL
Tel: 020 7501 4200 for stockists
www.malabar.co.uk
Upholstery fabrics at excellent prices. Good range of natural fibres. Plain fabrics in a variety of colours and textures, as well as stripes and checks

Olicana Textiles Ltd
Brook Mills, Crimble
Slaithwaite, Huddersfield
West Yorkshire HD7 5BQ
Tel: 01484 847666
Quality furnishing fabrics woven from natural yarns in plains, stripes, checks and neutrals; very reasonably priced

Pentonville Rubber
104/106 Pentonville Road
London N1 9JB
Tel: 020 7837 4582
www.pentonvillerubber.co.uk
Foam and rubber for upholstery, fillings for beanbags, cubes and poufs

Pongees
28–30 Hoxton Square
London N1 6NN
Tel: 020 7739 9130
www.pongees.co.uk
Silk specialists; a wide variety of weights, plus coloured parachute silks

Romo
Lowmoor Road, Kirkby-in-Ashfield
Nottingham NG17 7DE
Tel: 01623 750005 for stockists
Excellent range of plain colours in a variety of textures; I particularly like the range of cotton velvets

Russell & Chapple
68 Drury Lane
London WC2B 5SP
Tel: 020 7836 7521
www.randc.net
Canvas, cotton, muslin and linens, both dyed and natural, plus a wonderful green waterproof canvas for outdoors

Sanderson
Sanderson House
Oxford Road, Denham
Buckinghamshire UB9 4DX
Tel: 01895 830000 for stockists
www.sanderson-online.co.uk
Good cottons in stripes and checks and cotton velvets

Suasion
35 Riding House Street
London W1P 7PT
Tel: 020 7580 3763
Dyes and paints. A selection of natural fabric and ready-made items for dyeing

Texture
84 Stoke Newington Church Street
London N16 0AP
Tel: 020 7241 0990
www.textilesfromnature.com
*Eco-friendly fabrics including
organically grown cotton, hemp,
jute and recycled fabrics*

Wolfin Textiles Ltd
359 Uxbridge Road
Hatch End
Middlesex HA5 4JN
Tel: 020 8428 9111
www.wolfintextiles.co.uk
*Cotton, ticking, calico, muslin and
other utility fabrics, as well as cotton
and linen sheeting at low prices*

V. V. Rouleaux
6 Marylebone High Street
London W1M 3PB
Tel: 020 7224 5179 for branches
www.vvrouleaux.com
*Beautiful ribbons: cotton velvet in
bright greens and pink, especially
stylish; braids and trimmings*

Z. Butt Textiles
284 Brick Lane
London E1 6RL
Tel: 020 7247 7776
*Denim, silk, calico, white cotton drill,
muslin, all cheaper per metre if you
buy at least ten metres*

FURNITURE

Brick Lane
London E1 (Liverpool Street tube)
*Market held every Sunday morning:
catering equipment, factory tables and
chairs, office furniture, junk chairs,
tables, tablelinen and kitchenware*

Habitat
196 Tottenham Court Road
London W1P 9LD
Tel: 0645 334433 for nearest store
www.habitat.net
*Simple, modern and affordable tables
plus folding slatted white chairs for all
around the house*

Heal's
196 Tottenham Court Road
London W1P 9LD
Tel: 020 7896 7555 for branches
www.heals.co.uk
*Some good simple chairs and tables
for inside and outside*

Ikea
(see Fabrics for address details)
*Good value trestle table, solid pine
kitchen tables, basic chairs and stools.*

HOUSEHOLD LINENS

Ikea
(see Fabrics for address details)
*Great value cotton bath mats, towels
in good colours and shower curtains*

John Lewis
(see Fabrics for address details)
*The best place for white towels in
absorbent cotton textures, also shower
curtains in towelling and canvas*

The White Company
Unit 30 Perivale Industrial Park
Greenford
Middlesex UB6 7RJ
Tel: 0870 900 9555
www.thewhiteco.com
Simple yet stylish cotton towels

TABLEWARE

After Noah
121 Upper Street
London N1 1QP
Tel: 020 7359 4281
and
261 King's Road
London SW3 5EL
Tel: 020 7351 2610
www.afternoah.biz
*Retro kitchenware: schoolroom-style
glasses and chunky white mugs*

The Conran Shop
(see Fabric for address details)
*Plain white china, blue and white
striped Cornishware, simple wine
glasses and other functional tableware*

David Mellor
4 Sloane Square
London SW1W 8EE
Tel: 020 7730 4259 for mail order
www.davidmellordesign.com
*Excellent contemporary cutlery,
ceramics and glasses*

Divertimenti
33/34 Marylebone High Street
London W1U 4PT
Tel: 020 7935 0689
www.divertimenti.co.uk
*Good selection of cutlery, white china
and simple white serving dishes*

Habitat
(see Furniture for address details)
*Basic white china, simple cutlery, table-
cloths and napkins in bright colours*

Heal's
(see Furniture for address details)
*Beautiful white china and simple
cutlery*

Ikea
(see Fabric for address details)
*Unbeatable value tableware; white
china, basic tumblers, glasses and
cutlery*

Jerry's Home Store
80–81 Tottenham Court Road
London W1T 4TF
Tel: 020 7436 7177 for enquiries
Tel: 0870 840 6060 for mail order
www.jerryshomestore.com
*Linen tablecloths and napkins, as well
as cutlery and china*

John Lewis
(see Fabrics for address details)
*All the basics; white china, tablecloths,
simple cutlery and a range of blue
and white striped ceramics*

Lakeland Ltd
Alexandra Buildings
Windermere
Cumbria LA23 1BQ
Tel: 015394 88100 for mail order
www.lakelandlimited.com
*All kinds of kitchen tools and gadgets,
including cheap plastic storage boxes,
wooden spoon and food nets*

McCord
London Road
Preston
Lancashire PR11 1RP
Tel: 0870 908 7005
www.mccord.uk.com
*Galvanised or cream enamel jugs,
galvanised vases, simple white
ceramics and chunky glasses*

Robert Welch Designs
Lower High Street
Chipping Campden
Gloucestershire GL55 6DY
Tel: 01386 840522 for stockists
and mail order
www.welch.co.uk
*Classic simple cutlery in stainless
steel, also available to order in silver
plate and sterling silver*

Waterford Wedgwood
158 Regent Street
London W1B 5SW
Tel: 020 7734 7262
www.wedgwood.com
*Simple white bone china dinner
plates and tableware*

FOOD

Abbey Parks Asparagus
Abbey Parks Farm
East Heckington
Boston
Lincolnshire PE20 3QG
Tel: 01205 820722
www.abbeyparksasparagus.co.uk
*Fresh asparagus available by mail
order or from the farm shop*

Brindisa
32 Exmouth Market
London EC1R 4QE
Tel: 020 7713 1666
www.brindisa.com
*Jamon from free-range, acorn-fed
Black Foot pigs; Spanish cheeses,
olives, chickpeas, olive oil and bottled
tomatoes. They also have a weekly
stall at London's Borough Market*

Dell Farm
Painswick
Near Stroud
Gloucestershire GL6 6SQ
Tel: 01452 813382
*Naturally reared whole or half lambs
for the deep freeze*

**Fresh Olive Company of
Provence**
Unit 1
Hanover West Industrial Estate
Acton Lane
London NW10 7NB
Tel: 020 8453 1918 for enquiries
and mail order
www.fresholive.com
*Olives, oils, antipasti and vegetables
sourced from small family producers
all over France, Italy and Spain*

Jones Dairy
23 Ezra Street
London E2 7RH
Tel: 020 7739 5372
*Old-fashioned food shop selling
wonderful English cheeses, home-
made cheesecake, freshly ground
aromatic coffee, and bunches of
fresh herbs. Open 3 days a week*

London Farmers' Markets
PO Box 37363
London N1 7WB
Tel: 020 7704 9659
www.lfm.org.uk
Fruit, vegetables, meat, cheese, eggs, bread and homemade cakes direct from the producers. Visit their website to find your local farmers market

Henrietta Green's Food Lovers Britain
Henrietta Green
Food Lovers Fairs Ltd
Kilburn Park Road
London NW6 5LF
Tel: 020 7644 0455
www.foodloversbritian.com
Brainchild of foodie enthusiast Henrietta Green, who works tire-lessly to promote local produce and individual specialist suppliers. Her Food Lovers' Farmers Markets are held all over the country, where you can buy real meat from properly reared animals, and seasonal fruits and vegetables that actually taste like they should

Sierra Rica
C. La Julianita 7–9
Poligono Cantalgallo
Aracene 21200
Huelva
Spain
Tel: 00 34 959 127327
www.sierrarica.com for stockists
Organic foods from Andalucia, Southern Spain, including peeled and cooked chestnuts, membrillo, soups and cooking sauces

ECO-FRIENDLY PRODUCTS

Damhead Organic Foods
32a Damhead
Old Pentland Road
Lothianburn
Edinburgh
West Lothian EH10 7EA
Tel: 0131 448 2091 for mail order
www.damhead.co.uk
Eco-cleaning products such as washing-up liquid, bleach and kitchen roll

Energy Efficiency Advice Centre
136 Upper Street
London N1 1QP
Tel: 0800 512012 for branches
www.saveenergy.co.uk
Advice on how to save energy and money in the home

Green Building Store
11 Huddersfield Road
Meltham
Holmfirth
West Yorkshire HD9 4NJ
Tel: 01484 854898
www.greenbuildingstore.co.uk
Environmentally friendly loft insulation made from recycled newspapers; a non-toxic, solvent-free paint, varnish stripper, natural paints

Furniture Recycling Network
c/o Community Furniture Service
The Old Drill Hall
17a Vicarage Street North
Wakefield WF1 4JS
Tel: 0116 233 7007
Information about furniture recycling projects

Lakeland Ltd
(see Tableware for address details)
Recycling bird feeder, composting bins, carrier-bag bins, can crushers, airers

Natural Collection
Eco House, Monmouth Place
Bath BA1 2DQ
Tel: 0870 331 3333
www.naturalcollection.com
Eco-friendly products for all areas of the home by mail order; clockwork radios, organic sheets, clothes airers

ORGANIC GARDENING

Association Kokopelli
Ripple Farm
Crundale, Canterbury
Kent CT4 7EB
Tel: 0966 448379 / 01227 731815
www.organicseedsonline.com
Formerly Terre des Semences, a huge selection of organic seeds; varieties of tomatoes, peppers, pumpkins, sunflowers, lavender and alliums

crocus.co.uk ltd
Nursery Court, London Road
Windlesham
Surrey GU20 6LQ
Tel: 01344 629 629
www.crocus.co.uk
Varieties of sunflowers, hyacinths, agapanthus, alliums and amaryllis

David Austin Roses Ltd
Bowling Green Lane, Albrighton
Wolverhampton WV7 3HB
Tel: 01902 376300
www.davidaustinroses.com
Hundreds of varieties or roses; rambling, wild, old fashioned, bush and standard roses. Visit their large rose garden for inspiration

Groom Bros Ltd
Pecks Drove Nurseries
Clay Lake
Spalding
Lincolnshire PE12 6BJ
Tel: 01775 722421
www.grooms-flowers.co.uk
Good selection of bulbs for autumn and winter planting, including tulips and narcissi

Hardy's Cottage Garden Plants
Priory Lane
Freefolk Proirs
Whitchurch
Hampshire RG28 7NJ
Tel: 01256 896533
www.hardys-plants.co.uk
Specialist in herbaceous perennials; geraniums, irises, delphiniums and foxgloves

The Organic Gardening Catalogue
The Riverdene Business Park
Molesey Road
Hersham
Surrey KT12 4RG
Tel: 01932 253666
www.organiccatalog.com
Organic fertilisers, pest control solutions, composting bins, and a large choice of seeds including nasturtiums, sunflowers, foxgloves and broad beans

Author's acknowledgements

I would like to extend a big thank you to everyone who has collaborated on Sew Easy but especially to the team at Quadrille – Jane O'Shea, Helen Lewis, Lisa Pendreigh and Sue Storey, who have been supportive, inspiring and a joy to work with throughout.

Simon Wheeler's pictures are fabulous and truly original and Kate Storer has once again proved to be a creative genius with her illustrations and sewing skills. Thanks too to my brilliant agent, Clare Conville at Conville and Walsh.

Thank you also to Emma and Damon Heath, Richard and Sidonie Naylor, Jones Dairy; Fiona Wheeler for providing bed, board and emotional sustenance; Flowerstore.com at Liverpool Street Station and to our models: Fluffy canine London supermodel, Buttons and Puppy, Spain's hottest new furry face; Alice and Roisin Wheeler, twins Alice and Kate Hibberd; Tom, Georgie and Gracie Brown; bathroom cherub, Ishmail Dominguez; Hermione Tudor and dynamic Daisy.